THE PEOPLE'S VOICE
The development and current state of the South African small media sector

THE PEOPLE'S VOICE
The development and current state of the South African small media sector

Adrian Hadland & Karen Thorne
Commissioned by the Media Development and Diversity Agency

Compiled by the Social Integration and Cohesion Research Programme of the
Human Sciences Research Council, in partnership with the Media Development
and Diversity Agency and Mediaworks.

Published by HSRC Publishers
Private Bag X9182, Cape Town, 8000, South Africa
www.hsrcpublishers.ac.za

© 2004 Human Sciences Research Council

First published 2004

All rights reserved. No part of this book may be reprinted or reproduced or utilised
in any form or by any electronic, mechanical, or other means, including photocopying
and recording, or in any information storage or retrieval system, without permission
in writing from the publishers.

ISBN 0 7969 2059 1

Cover by Flame Design
Production by comPress

Distributed in Africa by Blue Weaver Marketing and Distribution,
PO Box 30370, Tokai, Cape Town, 7966, South Africa.
Tel: +27 +21-701-4477
Fax: +27 +21-701-7302
email: booksales@hsrc.ac.za

Distributed worldwide, except Africa, by Independent Publishers Group,
814 North Franklin Street, Chicago, IL 60610, USA.
www.ipgbook.com
To order, call toll-free: 1-800-888-4741
All other inquiries, Tel: +1 +312-337-0747
Fax: +1 +312-337-5985
email: Frontdesk@ipgbook.com

Printed by Creda Communications

Contents

List of abbreviations vi
Executive summary xi
Acknowledgements xv

Chapter 1: Small media in South Africa 1

1.1 Introduction 1
1.2 Opportunities and challenges 2
1.3 Research goals and objectives 5
1.4 Methodology 6
1.5 Assumptions and scope 8
1.6 Definition of community and independent media in South Africa 9

Chapter 2: Small media and the policy environment 19

2.1 Introduction 19
2.2 Community media and values 19
2.3 Overview of policy developments prior to 1994 26
2.4 Overview of policy developments: post-1994 32
2.5 Small media: the law, ethics and the regulators 41
2.6 Universal access and ICT policy 44
2.7 Small media: labour and skills development 46
2.8 Small media and the global experience 47
2.9 Parallel initiatives 51

Chapter 3: Overview of small media in South Africa 53

3.1 Introduction 53
3.2 Community radio 55
3.3 Print media 57
3.4 Community audiovisual media 59
3.5 The future: community multimedia services? 61
3.6 Conclusion 63

Chapter 4: Analysis and conclusions 65

4.1 Introduction 65
4.2 Human resource development 68
4.3 Institutional capacity building 75
4.4 Partnerships 79
4.5 Financial modelling 84
4.6 Networking and information 92
4.7 Content development 96
4.8 Technical sustainability 98
4.9 Further research 99

Chapter 5: Conclusion 101

Appendix: Questionnaires 103

References 123

LIST OF ABBREVIATIONS

ABC	Audit Bureau of Circulations
ABET	Adult Basic Education and Training
AEJMC	Association for Education in Journalism and Mass Communication
ANC	African National Congress
APA	Advertising Procurement Agency
ASA	Advertising Standards Authority
BCCSA	Broadcasting Complaints Committee of South Africa
BEE	Black Economic Empowerment
BITF	Black Information Technology Forum
CACs	Community arts centres
CAF	Communication Assistance Foundation
CALS	Centre for Applied Legal Studies, University of Witwatersrand
CBOs	Community based organisations
CEM	Community Electronic Multimedia
CEMI	Community Electronic Multimedia Indaba
CGE	Commission for Gender Equality
CIB	Campaign for Independent Broadcasting
CMS	Community Multimedia Services
CMSTT	Community Multimedia Services Task Team
Codesa	Convention for a Democratic South Africa
COM	Campaign for Open Media
Comnet	Community Media Network
Comtask	Task Group on Government Communication
Copssa	Community Print Sector of South Africa
Cosatu	Congress of South African Trade Unions
CPA	Community Print Association
CRIS	Communication Rights in the Information Society
CRWG	Community Radio Working Group
CSIR	Council for Scientific and Industrial Research
CSSA	Computer Society of South Africa
CTV	Community Television
CVET	Community Video Education Trust
DA	Democratic Alliance
DAC	Department of Arts and Culture
DACST	Department of Arts, Culture, Science and Technology
Danced	Danish Co-operation for Environment and Development (now DANIDA)
Danida	Danish International Development Assistance

LIST OF ABBREVIATIONS

DFID	Department for International Development, UK
DIP	Democratic Information Programme
DoC	Department of Communications
DP	Democratic Party
DPT	Department of Post and Telecommunications
DST	Department of Science and Technology
DTI	Department of Trade and Industry
EIF	Electronic Industries Federation
FAWO	Film and Allied Workers Organisation
FCJ	Forum for Community Journalists
FES	Frederich Ebert Stiftung
FPB	Film and Publications Board
FRU	Film Resource Unit
FXI	Freedom of Expression Institute
GATT	General Agreement on Tariffs and Trade
GCIS	Government Communication and Information System
GCPF	Government Communication Planning Forum
HRD	Human resource development
HSRC	Human Sciences Research Council
IBA	Independent Broadcasting Authority (later known as Icasa)
Icasa	Independent Communications Authority of South Africa
ICT	Information and Communication Technology
ICT-E	Information and Communication Technology and Electronics
Idasa	Institute for Democracy in South Africa
IDP	Integrated Development Plan
IDS	Integrated Development Strategy
IISA	Information Industry of South Africa
IIU	Infrastructure Investment Unit
IMA	Independent Media Association
IMDT	Independent Media Diversity Trust
ISAD	Information Society and Development
ISETT SETA	Information Systems, Electronic and Telecommunications Technologies Sector Education and Training Authority
ISRDS	Integrated Sustainable Rural Development Strategy
ITA	Information Technology Association
ITU	International Telecommunications Union
KZN C-VAC	KwaZulu-Natal Community Video Access Centre

THE PEOPLE'S VOICE

LISSC	Local Intersectoral Steering Committee
MAC	Media Advisory Committee
MAPPP SETA	Media, Advertising, Printing, Publishing and Packaging Sector Education and Training Authority
MCCC	Multimedia Community Communication Centre
MCU	Monitoring and Complaints Unit
MDDA	Media Development and Diversity Agency
MERS SETA	Manufacturing, Engineering and Related Services Sector Education and Training Authority
MIIU	Municipal Infrastructure Investment Unit
MISA	Media Institute of Southern Africa
MPA	Magazine Publishers Association of South Africa
MPCCs	Multi-purpose Community Centres
MTC	Media Training Centre
Mwasa	Media Workers Association of South Africa
NAB	National Association of Broadcasters
NAM	Non-Aligned Movement
NASA	Newspaper Association of Southern Africa
NCIS	National Communication and Information System
NCMF	National Community Media Forum
NCRF	National Community Radio Forum
Nemisa	National Electronic Media Institute of South Africa
Nepad	New Partnership for Africa's Development
NFVF	National Film and Video Foundation
NGO	Non-governmental organisation
NISSC	National Intersectoral Steering Committee
NIZA	Netherlands Institute vir Zuidelike Afrika
NLF	National Lottery Fund
NMEI	National Media Education Initiative
Norad	Norwegian Agency for Development Cooperation
NP	National Party
NQF	National Qualifications Framework
NTVA	National Television and Video Association
OSF	Open Society Foundation
OSISA	Open Society Initiative for South Africa
OWN	Open Window Network
Pansalb	Pan South African Language Board

LIST OF ABBREVIATIONS

PDU	Print Development Unit
PISSC	Provincial Intersectoral Steering Committee
PiT	Public Information Terminal
PMF	Print Media Forum
PMSA	Print Media South Africa
POSA	Press Ombudsman of South Africa
PTF	Provincial Telecentre Forum
RDP	Reconstruction and Development Programme
SABC	South African Broadcasting Corporation
SABPB	South African Broadcast Production Bodies
SACF	South African Communications Forum
Sacob	South African Chamber of Business
SACRIN	South African Community Radio Information Network
SACS	South African Communication Services
SADBAB	South African Digital Broadcasting Advisory Board
SAHRC	South African Human Rights Commission
SAIH	Norwegian Students and Academics International Assistance Fund
SAITIS	South African Industrial Strategy Project
Sanco	South African National Civics Organisation
Sanef	South African National Editors Forum
Sangoco	South African NGO Coalition
SAPA	South African Press Association
SAPAB	South African Production Advisory Body
SAQA	South African Qualifications Authority
SATRA	South African Telecommunications Regulatory Authority
SAUJ	South African Union of Journalists
SETA	Sector Education and Training Authority
SGB	Standards Generating Body
SITA	State Information Technology Agency
SMME	Small, Medium and Micro Enterprise
TBVC	Transkei, Bophuthatswana, Venda, Ciskei
TEC	Transitional Executive Committee
TELI	Technology Enhanced Learning Investigation
TTT	Technical Task Team on Broadcasting Policy
UN	United Nations
Unesco	United Nations Educational, Scientific, and Cultural Organisation
URP	Urban Renewal Programme

The people's voice

USA	Universal Service Agency
USF	Universal Service Fund
VRC	Video Resource Centre
WACC	World Association for Christian Communication
WIL	Web-Internet Laboratory
WSIS	World Summit on the Information Society
WTO	World Trade Organisation
WWR	Workers World Radio

Executive summary

This report provides an overview of the participants, policy, opportunities and challenges facing the community and independent media sector in South Africa at this time. The sector will be referred to collectively as small media in this report. The principal objective of the research was to provide the Media Development and Diversity Agency (MDDA) with new, current information, research and data to assist its rapid and effective intervention in the sector.

While this research was carried out to assist the MDDA, and has been substantially funded by the MDDA, it has been carried out independently. The findings and conclusions contained in this report do not reflect the MDDA's official position with regard to the sector, nor do they commit the MDDA to any particular course of action. Some of the suggestions made in this report fall beyond the ambit of the MDDA and are included to inform the sector's strategic thinking more broadly.

The MDDA was established in 2002 with the explicit objective of providing an enabling environment for the development of a diverse media. The MDDA, the board of which is appointed by Parliament, is intended to direct funding and support toward the sector in the interest of deepening South Africa's young democracy.

The last ten years has seen the publication of a series of reports on the small media sector including evaluations, conference proceedings, task group investigations and articles. Until now, these have not been brought together, assessed and analysed within one document. There is also much primary data that has been gathered specifically for this report that has not been documented before. The design of the research tools, the questionnaires and databases have all been done with the needs of the MDDA in mind and with its substantive input. The authors have, where possible, provided the MDDA with advance, preliminary results and data to assist in the urgent framing of funding criteria and other tasks.

The project started independently as a collaborative project of the Human Sciences Research Council (HSRC) and the NGO Mediaworks. The MDDA's board joined as a full partner in early 2003. The draft report and its conclusions were presented to the MDDA board in September 2003. The report itself is divided into four chapters.

Key elements of this report include the implications of convergence at a grassroots level on small media, finding common interests of small commercial media and community media and, most especially, a detailed examination of sustainability and how it can be fostered in this sector. A holistic view is taken of sustainability that is fleshed out by a number of specific conclusions and suggestions.

Chapter 1 gives an introduction to the sector, highlights some important opportunities and challenges and outlines the goals and objectives of the project. The chapter indicates the range of research outputs and details the underpinning methodology. The assumptions and scope of the research is also detailed. The chapter defines a number of concepts and concludes with a discussion of the importance and role of community media in the context of the media environment as a whole.

Chapter 2 concerns policy issues, both in South Africa and internationally. It gives the context to community media by citing the development of the global movement and by stating the values that underpin the sector. The chapter gives an overview of policy developments in the pre-1994 and post-1994 periods. It sets out legislation that has relevance to the sector as well as any administrative steps taken by government that are important. African policy initiatives are also outlined. The chapter describes the legal and ethical environment, considers the ambit of various regulators and examines information and communication technology policy. Within the chapter will be found a discussion of global trends and the experience of community media within different national contexts. Parallel initiatives, for instance in the telecommunications and education sectors, currently taking place in South Africa are set out.

Chapter 3 gives an overview of the community and independent media sector in South Africa as described in the collected data. The overall picture is of a sector that is struggling but which has enormous potential. One of the more interesting findings is the large number of community print media organisations operating in South Africa at present. This chapter sketches the distribution of the sector as a whole, provides a topography of service providers, presents key stakeholders, deals with community multimedia services and concludes with best practice recommendations on how to assess community communication needs.

Chapter 4 contains a detailed analysis of the collected data, questionnaires and literature and gives a total of 28 conclusions based on this research. In summarised form, these conclusions are as follows:

Conclusion 1: It is clearly important for the MDDA to target least-serviced areas and groups, particularly the rural parts of the country as well as providing access to the media to women and the disabled. But it is also vital to note that international best practice and the evidence of this research indicate that media organisations cannot simply be dropped into areas without a clear need being expressed by an already active group of organised people.

Conclusion 2: A national awareness campaign is necessary to illustrate the potential of small media. This should be dovetailed with the already existing National Media Education Initiative (NMEI).

Conclusion 3: While this research presents a hitherto unavailable topography of the sector, additional mapping procedures involving the South African Broadcasting Corporation (SABC) and other private media are necessary for a complete picture, in particular of under- and unserviced areas.

Conclusion 4: Where more than one community media organisation exists in the same area, moves should be made to merge or collaborate to prevent unnecessary competition for resources. This is also true of service providers.

Conclusion 5: Use should be made of already existing infrastructural or institutional resources, such as Multi-purpose Community Centres or telecentres, to locate future small media projects. This is in line with the thinking of the Community Multimedia Services Task Team (CMSTT).

Conclusion 6: An integrated human resource development (HRD) plan is essential for the small media sector. This process should be led by the MDDA.

Executive summary

Conclusion 7: A decade of media training nationwide has spawned many lessons. These should be acknowledged and taken forward. Some of these lessons are listed.

Conclusion 8: Qualifications around the needs of small media need to be customised as part of the National Qualifications Framework (NQF). This should be done in collaboration with sector service providers and higher education institutions.

Conclusion 9: The MDDA needs to clarify its anticipated role in the sector, particularly with regard to its relationship with networks and service providers.

Conclusion 10: A number of plans for provincial hubs are in the pipeline. This is a concept that needs to be explored by the MDDA with a view to creating larger centres of excellence for providing support to small media in all the country's provincial areas.

Conclusion 11: A management service to facilitate institutional support and development for small media needs to be established. The service would provide management services such as human resource policies, loan application assistance, taxation and administrative help, research methodology and the production of a handbook on managing volunteers.

Conclusion 12: A website and manual needs to be created to provide access to the management service listed in Conclusion 11 but also to provide a range of useful materials and resources to small media organisations. These resources might include contract templates, examples of advertising rate cards, legal documents and form letters.

Conclusion 13: The MDDA needs to be flexible about what it considers community media as ownership structure is not always the best indication of the closeness of ties between a local media organisation and the community it serves.

Conclusion 14: Convergence has serious implications for strategies adopted by the MDDA. Understanding the dynamics of convergence and their impact must rank as an important policy priority. Communication and co-operation with the CMS task team is advised.

Conclusion 15: The relationship between small media and government is complex and largely ill-defined. Various strategies are proposed for clarifying the roles and responsibilities of this relationship, including the drawing up of a code of practice and the lobbying of various government departments to use small media outlets.

Conclusion 16: A marketing procurement agency should be established to facilitate access by small media to government communications contracts.

Conclusion 17: An ethical and mutually beneficial partnership should be established between the mainstream media, including public and private broadcasters, and small media.

Conclusion 18: Funding channels to small media require improved co-ordination and information sharing. Various options are proposed to assist in synergising government funding to the sector in particular.

Introduction

Conclusion 19: Funding priorities are suggested in light of the research undertaken including the recommendation that cash handouts be balanced with sector wide interactions aimed at building the sustainability of small media.

Conclusion 20: Partnerships and resource sharing should be encouraged both between small media organisations and between small media organisations and 'like-minded' or relevant local structures.

Conclusion 21: Project management, and in particular the management of partnerships, needs to be built into training interventions as a matter of priority.

Conclusion 22: The authors propose a range of sustainability strategies, including research into a national advertising procurement agency, a new system for circulation verification, a new arrangement for printing procurement, the securing of a discounted rate for connectivity and the establishment of a sectoral investment institution.

Conclusion 23: A common wish was expressed throughout the sector for more information in the form of a regularly updated electronic news and information service. Other information needs are listed including information on policy and regulatory developments, best practice models, public health information, skills development, funding opportunities and government tenders.

Conclusion 24: Findings on proposed roles for the MDDA, government, the national networks and service providers are set out, as described by the major sectoral service providers.

Conclusion 25: Independent and community media networks need to be strengthened.

Conclusion 26: A national news agency for small media needs to be investigated.

Conclusion 27: A technology plan for the small media sector needs to be drawn up. This requires an investigation into appropriate, adaptable, compatible, user-friendly hardware and software to inform purchase choices for the sector.

Conclusion 28: A maintenance plan for community radio stations needs to be developed. This should be done in collaboration with the National Community Radio Forum (NCRF) and the Department of Communications (DoC).

A number of suggestions for further research are included in the report.

ACKNOWLEDGEMENTS

The authors would like to thank the following for their assistance and co-operation with this project: the small media organisations, funding bodies and sector service providers who painstakingly and patiently filled out our questionnaires, responded to our queries and put up with our demands on their time and staff; the NCRF and Agenda for assistance with the case studies; Martin Stevens and Bukelwa Voko; Erika Lundstrom and Hanna Fransson, the two Swedish Masters students who helped pilot some of the questionnaires; Nuraan Amlay who did much of the hard work in collecting and ordering the data; Kristin Klose of the GCIS; Jackie Cameron for proofreading and to the staff and administrators of both the HSRC's Social Cohesion and Integration Research Programme and Mediaworks.

The work has been funded in part by the South African Parliament through its baseline funding of HSRC research projects and by the MDDA which made an early funding grant to expand and focus the work.

The authors would like to thank the Open Society Foundation for contributing to the initial stage of this project when it was still envisaged as a survey of the needs and conditions of community media in the Northern, Western and Eastern Cape for Mediaworks.

1 SMALL MEDIA IN SOUTH AFRICA

> *Never doubt that a small group of thoughtful, committed citizens can change the world; indeed, it's the only thing that ever has.*
>
> *Margaret Mead*

1.1 Introduction

The establishment of the Media Development and Diversity Agency (MDDA) was the result of more than ten years of discussion, planning and negotiation. It has the potential to be a profound moment in the development of South Africa's media and in the enrichment and deepening of the country's democratic way of life. Few who are involved in the small media sector will dispute the considerable challenges and obstacles that face them. Questions of sustainability, appropriate technology, management skills, human resources development, sector co-ordination, policy integration and globalisation, to name a few, plague planners as much as they constrain media organisations themselves.

There is the overwhelming conviction both domestically and globally that a vibrant small media sector represents an essential component of sustainable development and a stable democracy and is a critical catalyst for the improvement of ordinary people's lives. Support for the sector and its role can be found in virtually all major policy pronouncements emanating not only from South Africa's current ruling party and government but from major multilateral organisations such as the United Nations (UN). There is a large degree of consensus, in other words, concerning the importance of the small media sector. Equally, there is agreement that South Africa's media landscape some ten years after the advent of democracy is, in ownership terms, considerably less diverse than it should be.

There is far less unanimity over the specific strategies needed to develop and support small media. The debate seems to have polarised around a 'market-driven' stance, in which small media sink or swim based on the exigencies of the market, versus a more developmental approach that assumes a degree of baseline support is a prerequisite for sustainability. The suggestions contained in this report present a pragmatic middle ground.

This research includes reference to the ongoing debates, both locally and internationally, that have sprung up around the notion of community media and its role in society and within the media as a whole. The MDDA will need, in time, to make up its own collective mind on its attitude to these issues.

We intend to present a range of practical strategies based on newly updated data and on the existing accumulated knowledge in the sector, that will provide options on the way forward. We hope that this will assist the MDDA to 'hit the road running' and fulfil its role expeditiously.

For the purposes of expediency, the rather long-winded phrase 'community and independent media' will be referred to in this report as 'small media' except where either community media (that is, non-profit) or the independent media (that is, small, commercial) are referred to specifically. Visually the small media sector can be represented as shown in Figure 1.

Figure 1: The small media sector

1.2 Opportunities and challenges

In broad terms, the small media sector finds itself facing a range of new dynamics and trends, both threatening and presenting enormous opportunities for growth and development.

1.2.1 Participatory democracy and sustainable development

Certainly the emergence and deepening of a new democratic era in South Africa with its emphasis on transparency, accountability, accessibility, empowerment and equity is essential to the core principles and basic objectives of the small media sector. The link, too, between sustainable development, empowerment and the small media sector has been demonstrated in country after country.

Global experts are emphatic that a diverse, independent media is an essential component of a healthy democracy. In South Africa during the apartheid era, the small media more than played its part in exposing human rights abuses by the state and in giving a voice to the voiceless. Now the challenge has shifted. In a democratic state, the challenge for community and independent media will be to deepen their role. In reality, many community and independent media organisations have failed to come to grips with their roles in community development and in promoting participatory democracy. They have often not developed sufficient ties with civic structures that would bring them closer to the communities they serve. While committed to creating content for development and empowerment purposes, they also often lack the skills and resources to make any real impact in this respect.

'Tensions over the delivery of social services is one of the primary fault lines of South Africa today,' the Freedom of Expression Institute (FXI) argues, pointing at ongoing friction within the ANC alliance and the emergence of social movements increasingly critical of government lack of delivery (FXI Annual report 2001/2002).[1] These forces are bound to confront the small media sector as it seeks to act as a vehicle of citizen communication. The question must be asked whether, and to what extent, the political will exists to create a truly equitable and free media environment, which is accessible by citizens and civil society organisations, some of which may be critical of government policies? This is particularly relevant in the case of community television, which has been on the policy backburner for many years.

1.2.2 Technology and convergence

Advances in technology are making it possible for small media to leapfrog traditional media and embrace digital technology, which is low cost, high quality and easy to use. This creates opportunities for small media to use all forms of media across one digital platform. This approach is already evident in many innovative projects countrywide which are providing community access to combinations of radio, print, information services, Information and Communication Technologies (ICTs), video and indeed more traditional forms of communication such as the performing and visual arts.

This creates the opportunity to build small media on the country's information backbone and is linked to extensive government efforts to promote 'universal access' to ICTs.

---

1 http://www.fxi.org.za

Indeed, what is increasingly referred to as Community Multimedia Services (CMS) are starting to emerge in the context of telecentres, Multi-purpose Community Centres (MPCCs), youth centres and community arts centres (CACs).

This media convergence encourages the building of partnerships between local stakeholders towards the achievement of locally identified needs. It is dependent on resource-mapping and results in the effective utilisation of limited local resources. By extension, it encourages phased or incremental development of media skills and objectives, starting out with achievable 'small steps' such as low-tech print media production, basic newsletter production and community notice boards (while the wait, in some instances, is seven years for a radio licence).

While the impact of convergence between telecommunications, computers and broadcasting has still to be felt, it is important that small media is not left behind. Strategic positioning at an early phase will ensure small media gains a critical advantage and can make the most of its location on the cusp of a new communications era. But convergence has already caught more than a few napping. According to media commentator Tracey Naughton: 'The community media sector's attempts to develop its own survival are being compounded by an era of convergence that is moving far too quickly for the country's stage of development' (Naughton 1999: 6). Convergence, in other words, presents many opportunities to the small media sector, but many dangers too. The possibilities of new, cheap multi-media platforms and easily accessible, quality content are potentially counterbalanced by the presence of policy vacuums, overlaps, duplication and inter-departmental competition.

1.2.3 Policy, legislation and implementation

As far back as 1979, media analysts began to talk of the phenomenon of convergence and of how it was becoming hard to compartmentalise the hitherto autonomous information platforms of print, broadcast and telecommunications (Jankowski, Prehn & Stappers 1992). What intrigued policy planners in the 1970s has become a powerful, even pervasive force in the opening period of the twenty-first century. The rules have simply changed and are changing with ceaseless rapidity. Digitisation, broadband technology, satellites and the Internet have had far-reaching and frequently unpredicted impacts. In most cases, the technology has moved faster than either the regulators or the law.

The extraordinary pace of change has blurred the lines of responsibility between governments and between their departments. This is far from unique to South Africa. Policies that are refined by one ministry have to be implemented by others. Strategies are frequently poorly co-ordinated. The change has made regulators' work difficult and, at times, even impossible.

The convergence of technologies has corresponded with the elevation of information as a fundamental constituent of economic development. This has, in turn, seen the placement of communication and information needs at the top of government political agendas and as the key elements of economic and industrial policies. The consequence of this has been that more and more components of government at different tiers have a vested interest in harnessing information and communication technologies to achieve their own sectoral objectives.

As influential as convergence has been, it is still true that print, radio, television and multimedia occupy different spheres, with different histories and contexts. Broadcasting has generally led the way in South African policy terms and has frequently set the agenda on small media questions. Regulations and controls may, however, differ markedly from one form of media to the next. The extent to which they are each affected by the general and specific policy environments will be the subject of the next chapter of this report.

1.2.4 Macroeconomic environment

The Print Development Unit (PDU), an agency funded by the mainstream media, which provides assistance to small print media organisations, cites the emergence of a black middle class and rapid urbanisation as potential growth opportunities for emerging small media. As stable as South Africa's macroeconomic environment may be, the extremely high levels of unemployment, poverty and inequity will be felt most keenly at exactly the level at which small media operates.

A harsh economic environment will inevitably put pressure on organisations that are largely marginal operations. In such circumstances, advertising is difficult to attract, volunteers are hard to keep and resources are scarcer than ever. Of the 25 case studies featured in this report, half of the media organisations reported that they were 'struggling to survive' and half agreed that they were 'covering costs but had no room for growth' (see Chapter 3).

The FXI has shown how advertising levels (adspend) in South Africa have fallen in recent years, placing additional pressure on struggling media enterprises. According to Allister Sparks, the advertising industry is also 'deeply conservative' and resistant to change in accommodating community media's demands for recognition and for appropriate levels of adspend (Sparks 2003: 92).

User-churn – the extent to which consumers are falling out of the communications network due principally to a lack of affordability – is pronounced in telecommunications. Almost two-thirds of the Telkom phones installed in 2000 were disconnected as users couldn't pay spiralling costs, according to the FXI (FXI Annual report 2001/2002: 8).[2]

1.2.5 Human resource development

Considerable opportunities now loom in the area of human resource development (HRD) with the implementation of the National Qualifications Framework (NQF). Learnerships, for instance, recognise the kind of non-formal and work-based training that has always characterised the small media sector. Opportunities exist for tapping into the skills fund to sustain this kind of work and to develop unit standards thus engendering a participatory and community-oriented approach to media training. Standing in the way of these opportunities is NQF that is bureaucratic, slow and notoriously difficult to access.

The challenges in HRD are enormous. All existing research points to the need for training that incorporates governance, management, content creation and technical operations. There is no shortage of service providers (close to 30 nationally), skills and resources. But there is a great deal of duplication and a lack of co-ordination (see service provider analysis later in this report). The challenge will be to devise and implement an integrated human resource strategy for the sector.

---

2 http://www.fxi.org.za

The Employment Equity Act and other pressures on the mainstream media to transform also present enormous opportunities for redressing imbalances in the media through the entry of previously disadvantaged individuals into the media industry. In the absence of accessible and affordable training opportunities for many South Africans, small media has become an entry-level training ground for a new generation of aspirant media practitioners.

While the PDU encourages such 'staff exchange' and further suggests a 'Code of Practice', to govern it, the National Community Radio Forum (NCRF) has repeatedly stressed that this amounts to a critical brain drain from an already struggling sector.

1.2.6 Globalisation

The threat of globalisation is starkly felt in the media sector in a variety of ways. It is most keenly experienced in the continuing concentration of media ownership, in the dominance of transnational corporate agendas and in the gathering power of American cultural hegemony. Most at risk from these forces are indigenous cultural expression, pluralism and the right to communication.

The potential impact of these trends include the 'dumbing-down' of news and educational programming forms, a reduction in real content diversity and the undue influence of commercial imperatives on the news, current affairs and in educational content. Another effect is a growing disparity of access to information and communication technologies and applications globally, between urban and rural communities and between groups within society. The imposition of a single dominant set of cultural values and the domination of a single language are also worrying trends.

Against this background, in the clutch of powerful, global forces and in the face of almost overwhelming local odds, the community media sector in South Africa continues to survive. Millions of people garner vital information from the newsletters, talk shows and bulletins that characterise the sector's output. Thousands of ordinary people find skills, meaning and a sense of identity through the various media, often giving freely of their own time to gain little more than an opportunity to be heard. It is in the hope of giving encouragement and support to such people in the broader national interest that this project was devised.

1.3 Research goals and objectives

This research project was conceived in the latter half of 2002 with the principal objective of assisting the MDDA in starting its important and challenging work as quickly and efficiently as possible. Initially a collaboration between Mediaworks and the Human Sciences Research Council (HSRC), the MDDA became a full partner in the research early in 2003. Research instruments, such as questionnaires and databases, were tailored specifically to meet the needs and requirements of the MDDA.

Much has been researched, written and said about the importance of and need to develop community and independent media in South Africa. It was not the intention of the researchers to reinvent the wheel but rather to tap into this body of knowledge, to fill in the gaps and extrapolate the lessons learned. It was also our intention to highlight key strategies, describe the challenges and opportunities and promote further debate. On a more practical level, this project was designed to undertake a much-needed and simple data capturing exercise depicting 'who is out there?' or, perhaps more appropriately, 'what's left?' after years of neglect.

Our research goals are to:
- Promote media diversity by assisting the MDDA with key data, information and expert analysis that will inform the agency's work and contribute to the rapid realisation of its goals and work.
- Encourage strategic partnerships between relevant roleplayers to enhance co-ordination and prevent duplication in the sector.
- Examine the dynamics and financial modelling of the independent and community media sector with a view to promoting sustainability.
- Give community-based media projects the opportunity to share information on the opportunities and challenges they face.
- Facilitate information-sharing among community-based projects, service providers and, networks and funders on the environment in which they are working.

The outcomes include:
- A report containing:
    - An overview of the current topography and status of local media in South Africa today;
    - An overview of the policy and regulatory environment as it relates to the development of local media;
    - A background to the definition and rationale of community media in the South African and in the international context;
    - An analysis of the funding environment, including recommendations on targeted funding interventions;
    - An analysis of the sector's capacity enhancement needs and current activities and suggestions for designing an integrated human resource development strategy and other capacity enhancement interventions;
    - An analysis of existing networking, co-ordination and information dissemination arrangements in the sector and recommendations around how these may be improved;
    - An overview of international experience and best practice in the fields of community media policy and practice which is integrated throughout the document;
    - Some suggestions for accessing under-serviced areas based on a mapping exercise; and
    - Recommendations on further research that may be required.
- A national database of South African community and independent media organisations and service providers.

1.4 Methodology

The database was put together using existing databases from a wide range of sources, including the Independent Communications Authority of South Africa (Icasa), the National Association of Broadcasters (NAB), NCRF, PDU, the Independent Media Association (IMA), Government Communication and Information System (GCIS), together with person-to-person structured discussions with representatives of community and independent media organisations in order to verify details. While this is the most comprehensive list to date, there may well be developments in the sector that have not been recorded and therefore could not be included. Organisations were asked 19 basic questions including the name of the project, type of legal entity, contact details, composition of staff, infrastructure, target groups and geographic radius, language used, annual budget and sources of income. The database has been passed on to the MDDA.

In the course of this research, in-depth person-to-person interviews were conducted with the senior representatives of 25 small media organisations, representing a national, cross-section of print, radio and multimedia in urban and rural contexts. The interviews were based on questionnaires designed and piloted by the authors of this report and conducted by experienced media trainers and facilitators on-site.

The organisations that participated in the case study analysis are:
- Riviersonderend Advice and Development Centre, Riviersonderend, Western Cape;
- Indonsakusa Community Radio (Icora FM), Eshowe, KwaZulu-Natal;
- Unitra Community Radio, Umtata, Eastern Cape;
- Khanya Community Radio, Butterworth, Eastern Cape;
- Phatsima Youth Initiative, Upington, Northern Cape;
- Qhamani Youth Media Group, De Aar, Western Cape;
- Club Coffee Bar Community Centre, Oudtshoorn, Western Cape;
- Senzokhuhle CBO Networks, Eshowe, KwaZulu-Natal;
- Molweni CRC (greater), Linkhills, KwaZulu-Natal;
- Hartebeeskraal Multi-purpose Community Centre, Atlantis, Western Cape;
- Ubuntu News, Aliwal North, Eastern Cape;
- Radio Zibonele, Khayelitsha, Western Cape;
- Alexsan Resource Centre, Alexandra, Gauteng;
- Mohodi FM, Manthata, Limpopo;
- George Community Media Centre, George, Western Cape;
- Radio KC, Paarl, Western Cape;
- Hassequa Development Forum, Riversdale, Western Cape;
- Radio Mafisa, Rustenburg, North West;
- Neledi Community Radio, Senekal, Free State;
- Lentswe Community Radio, Parys, Free State;
- Vaaltar Community Radio, Taung, North West;
- Alex FM, Bramley, Gauteng;
- Witbank Community Radio, Witbank, Limpopo;
- Greater Middleburg Community Radio, Mhluzi, Mpumalanga
- Moletsi Community Radio, Polokwane, Northern Province; and
- Iliha Community Radio Station, Maclear, Eastern Cape.

Seven of the organisations are rural, three urban, eight are peri-urban and six are both rural and urban. Most (21) of the organisations are well established while three are newly 'emerging'. It is the authors' belief that the case studies collectively provide a detailed and authentic picture of conditions on the ground for community organisations in South Africa. Analysis of the case studies can be found in Chapter 3.

THE PEOPLE'S VOICE

A large group of service providers were also contacted and provided with questionnaires. These questionnaires were collated and are analysed within the body of this report (Chapter 3).

An overview of community media-related policy was compiled over the period of several months during early 2003. The overview examines all policy and legislation that appears to be relevant to the small media sector. A detailed timeline of relevant policy events is also included. A comprehensive resource pack of relevant literature – consisting of several lever-arch files – has been forwarded to the MDDA for reference.

A literature overview has been built into several sections of the report but is principally found in the sections on policy and on the global environment.

A survey of the funding environment was built into the service provider and case study questionnaires. In addition, the researchers interviewed key funders, both past and present.

While a considerable amount of effort, experience and insight has been marshalled into the production of this report, including interviews with roleplayers from one end of South Africa to the other, it is worth stating that this is merely an opening gambit in a longer-term endeavour. There is a great deal more research to be done on a multiplicity of fronts. Indeed, an important part of the MDDA's work will be to identify and commission this research to ensure the best enabling environment possible is put into place for the blooming of the small media.

Nevertheless, the researchers are confident that, together, the various elements of this report will collectively fulfil their primary purpose: to provide the MDDA with a good grasp of the current topography of the small media sector in South Africa as well as the tools and insights it requires to help design and implement its own interventions.

1.5 Assumptions and scope

While this research project sets out to paint a picture of the current state of the small media sector in South Africa and to present the results of a recent data collection and analysis process, a number of assumptions underpin this report that the authors feel need to be declared.

We do not intend to restate commonly-known information and/or assumptions. It is assumed, for instance, that the MDDA is familiar with its own founding legislation and the tasks and duties that emanate out of this. We will not be spelling this out again in detail.

We do note that the MDDA has been mandated to find solutions to the following key obstacles:
- Globalisation and concentration of ownership, homogenisation of the news;
- Failure of empowerment groups to acquire and sustain interests/shares in commercial media enterprises;
- Low density of media infrastructure, urban bias;
- Lack of resources to support growth;
- Legacy in media organisations of inadequate education and training;
- Illiteracy;

- Failure to promote indigenous languages;
- The promotion of development-oriented news and information; and
- Rapid development of new media and new skills and greater access to telecommunications.

Our other assumptions are as follows:
- We do not intend to outline the exact position with regard to concentration of ownership of the mainstream media in South Africa and assume that the patterns outlined in the MDDA's Draft Position Paper remain relevant.
- We do not intend to demonstrate the degree to which ordinary South Africans are under-served by access to the media, as this too has been detailed in other policy work.
- It is the authors' assumption that the inequities outlined in the report cited above remain, including with regard to resource allocation and to multilingual, cultural and educational programming, the lack of diversity and choice and the shortfall in universal coverage and access.
- The authors have placed a special emphasis on the community media including print, radio, video and multimedia and small commercial publishers. We have, however, excluded the independent film, video and radio sector as they do not appear to fall within the ambit of the MDDA's funding criteria.
- The authors acknowledge there is slightly more emphasis on print and audiovisual media than on the community radio sector in this report. This was intended to address the need for more information about the print and audiovisual sector as expressed in the MDDA position paper. The authors note that there is much information available on the community radio sector. The sector is well represented in the case studies, the database, the analysis and in other key sections of this report.

1.6 Definition of community and independent media in South Africa

Introduction

Our research indicates that there are wide-ranging interpretations about what small media is and, in particular, about the difference between community and independent media. In their book *New Publishers*, the PDU argues for the collapse of community and independent print media into the term 'new publishers' so as to 'avoid confusion between entrepreneurial publications and the non-profit, non-commercial "community press", (2002: 7). The authors of this report believe, however, that 'new publishers' is not an appropriate term. The reasons are as follows:
- Firstly, many South African community media organisations, such as Community Video Education Trust (CVET) and even Mediaworks, have been around since the late 1970s and early 1980s and can hardly be defined as 'new'. Community media are not a new phenomenon – not in South Africa, or elsewhere in the world. Community radio was established in Europe and in the United States as far back as the 1940s.
- Secondly, the catch-all phrase shows a lack of understanding of the role and definition of community media as developed through years of theory and practice, worldwide.
- Finally, the umbrella term 'new' obscures the vital difference between the community media sector and the independent media, which is a crucial distinction in policy terms.

The people's voice

Our understanding of community media is premised on the belief that all citizens have the 'right to communicate'. This right implies that citizens are offered access to community media to express their concerns, needs and, through dialogue, find common solutions to local problems. The notion of community media is not a euphemism for 'media for black people', as some might suggest. Community media 'enables the opinions and positions of the marginalised to be presented along, and challenge, the authoritative voice of the mainstream media' (Scott 1997: 3). The local focus of community media allows it to communicate directly with and through its participating communities.

Independent media, on the other hand, is privately-owned, commercial media which is free of control and influence by corporate or government interests (Community Media 2000, conference handbook cited in Naughton 1999). While small, independent media often target a defined geographic community or community of interest, it is not owned or controlled by that community, nor are they necessarily 'participatory' in nature. Our research findings indicate that many independent media represent the interests of a religious, ethnic or other 'segment' of the community, as opposed to having a mandate to meet the needs of the diverse population.

Independent media contribute to democracy by proliferating the diversity of voices heard in the media. In this respect there is no doubt that the independent media encourage debate and provide access to information with a 'localised' focus. However, the independents also have their limitations. They are usually driven by a commercial imperative as opposed to a social or developmental mandate. As a result, independent media will usually target more affluent markets. This focus does have a marked and positive influence on the financial sustainability of this sector but obviously limits the independent media's capacity to service, for instance, marginalised communities.

A useful comparison to illustrate the distinction between community and independent media is the example of public versus private broadcasting. Private broadcasters exist, first and foremost, to grow equity. The need to deliver audiences to advertisers means private broadcasters focus on entertainment and make use of a high proportion of cheap, imported content. Within these constraints, a diversity of voices and of ownership is promoted, usually through regulation. Equally, the private broadcasting sector has proven a useful vehicle for black economic empowerment.

Public broadcasting, on the other hand, has as its *raison d'etre* the provision of information, education and entertainment for the public. But it also has a whole host of other social and developmental objectives such as language diversity and nation building. Naturally it has to be sustainable. As a result, subsidies are provided to the public broadcaster to enable it to focus on its developmental mandate.

The community media, like the public broadcaster, has an over-riding developmental mandate. As with public broadcasting, the government recognises that subsidies are necessary to help local media fulfil this mandate. Similarly, the local, commercial media will ultimately sink or swim in the competitive market environment in which it has chosen to operate (Calabrese 1991: 123 cited in Berger 1996: 8).[3]

---

3 Conference paper, Community Voices Conference, see http://www.journ.ru.ac.za

Any consideration of community media has to start with three basic questions:
- What is a community?
- How does one define community media?
- Why is the community media considered important?

As fundamental as these questions are, there is no unanimity on most of the answers. It is necessary, however, to sketch the debates as they have an impact on the role, composition and future of the community media sector in South Africa.

1.6.1 What is a community?

The word 'community' has become one of the most useful buzzwords of the information age (Calabrese 1991: 123 cited in Berger 1996: 8). But its very usefulness serves, at times, to conceal its true meaning. According to Calabrese, 'by assigning ... projects with the label "community" we gut the term of anything resembling its philosophical meaning, and we delude ourselves into thinking that what is being achieved ... resembles anything like a voluntary commitment to sustaining communal life' (Jankowski et al. 1992 and Calabrese: 123 in Berger 1996: 8).

It was the influential media theorist Benedict Anderson who came up with the concept in the 1980s of the 'imagined community' (1983: 49). This was a community that, in effect, was created and sustained as a consequence of the workings and networks of the mass media. No longer could communities be viewed as a relatively small group of people living in close proximity.

Since then, the era of ICTs has spawned new notions of community, such as the virtual community and the reality community, that are even further removed from the geographic or physical markers which first defined the concept. Globalisation, too, has heralded the emergence of transnational communities, interest groups and social movements.

In addition, debates around what constitutes a community have a different dimension in the African context. According to one United Nations Educational, Scientific, and Cultural Organization (Unesco) report, the 'nation-building' that has characterised most post-colonial states has required the erosion of small community identities in order to deter potential conflict (Opubor 2000: 11). In the post-independence era, 'attempts were made to build societies that were broad-based, with centralised political power and authority and homogenised institutions, so as to emphasise commonalities and to incorporate disparate cultures in an effort to create "national unity"'(11). The consequence has been the creation of ever-larger political and economic units (such as the Southern African Development Community and the African Union) that have tended to bypass the ideas, opinions and direct contributions of the majority of citizens.

The definition of what constitutes a community is, therefore, contested. For Opubor, a community is built on the exchange of initiatives, information and meanings in the process of defining, creating and maintaining a group identity and in the interests of survival within a specific geographic and/or cultural space (2000: 13). Many other definitions abound, though, including that a community is merely a body of individuals or an organised political, municipal or social body.

The people's voice

In a work entitled *Communities of Tomorrow*, Stevenson disputes the idea that a community is principally defined by its homogeneity (2002: 737). Communities, he argues, are made up of people with different needs, views and identities. He cites Ingrid Burkett who argues in her work that 'community as homogeneity too easily denies difference and assimilation of the Other' (Burkett in Stevenson 2002: 737). Stevenson suggests that the 'art of co-operation' defines a community rather than the similarity of those who agree or choose to co-operate. As Burkett then explains: 'A community is a paradoxical experience. It is about difference as much as unity. It is about conflict and harmony, selfishness and mutuality, separateness and wholeness, discomfort and contentment. Privileging one of these opposites in interpreting communities denies the transforming powers of human communion and resorts to fixed ideas about communities' (Burkett in Stevenson 2002: 738).

South Africa too presents a far from neutral understanding of the term community. It's 'a PC (politically correct) synonym for underprivileged black people', argues Jeffrey Stevens (1997: 3) 'The word community is too politically loaded to be of any descriptive use' (3). Stevens adds that, in any case, communities are often imaginary, unstable and contradictory as well as dynamic and changing. For Louw, the problematic term 'community' has 'tended to become rhetorical in the South African context' (1993: 72). He suggests that 'community should refer to people in a particular local area who share similar problems and interests as a collectivity. In getting together to solve their joint problems, a community is created' (72). At virtually every level, the definition of a community and how it is comprised is subject to debate.

Media analyst Ole Prehn notes that a degree of consensus was achieved in media theory toward the notion that the production of media (and airing of programming) which was authentic and which presented real personal experience was only possible in a limited geographic area, even when the issues were translocal. 'The concept "community" was accordingly interpreted both as a "community area" and "a community of interest"' (Jankowski et al. 1992: 259).

This consensual position is one that finds expression within the Independent Broadcasting Authority (IBA) Act of 1993. The Act identifies two categories of community: a geographic community and a community of interest. The latter group could include institutional communities (such as trade unions, religious or cultural) which share common interests or goals.

The Act assumes a community is 'any group of persons or sector of the public having a specific ascertainable common interest'. The assumption, though, is far from uncontested. In the preparation of the Act there was considerable disagreement among key interest groups. At the time the Convention for a Democratic South Africa (Codesa) drew up the IBA Bill, (the interim) government supported the geographic/community of interest definition, business pushed for the non-profit notion and the mass democratic movement was keen on the community-controlled and community-owned dimension (Urgoiti 1999: 8). While a compromise was reached in the Act, many of the debates continue over the definitions. As Unesco has noted, the question of what a community is has 'still not (been) agreed upon' (Opubor 1999: 23).

1.6.2 What is community media?

> For the community, by the community, through the community
> *Broadcasting Policy Technical Task Team 1998*

Community media has its beginnings in the post-war world of the 1940s, more often than not as a vehicle of protest and of challenge. In North and South America as well as in many parts of Europe, community radio shrugged off the constraints of governmental and economic power to articulate the opinions, views and culture of ordinary people. Community print and community television have proven similarly inclined, offering a counterpoint to the globalisation, commercialisation and threatening homogeneity of what has become known as the information age.

Community media is the third of three components of the media, public, private and community, which dominate most countries' definition of what constitutes the sector. The public media refers mainly to radio and television and means public ownership, usually with state control. The private media operate within the free market and compete for audiences and advertising with a commercial, profit-oriented mandate. In South Africa, small private media is known as the independent media.

Community media is entirely different to the other two components. It provides the means for cultural expression, community discussion and debate. It supplies news and information and facilitates political engagement. It offers concrete means for public participation and for defending cultural diversity. Through access to the production and consumption of relevant communications, community media forms a collective platform for community empowerment (CRIS 2003).[4]

Some argue that the global community media sector is currently engaged in a struggle for ordinary people's rights to communicate and presents a vital barrier to the potentially destructive aspects of the information society: 'Much has been promised by the information society – access to vital knowledge for health and education, better information from governments and corporations, electronic democracy, global trade and exchange, up to the minute news. But because they lack the resources to make their voices heard in this shifting social landscape, the world's poorest communities face the twin dangers of being left out of this new economy and becoming a cultural dumping ground for mass market products made by and for the richest economies' (CRIS 2003).

Over the years, however, the notion of community media has come to incorporate a range of qualities and conditions that continue to distinguish it from the mainstream, public or independent media. It is important to characterise these distinguishing features.

According to the *St James Encyclopedia of Popular Culture*, community media is simply giving 'everyday people' access to the instruments of radio, television and computer-mediated communication (Howley 2002).[5] It is clear, however, that community media involves much more even than access merely to these instruments. A convincing case can be made, for instance, that puppetry constitutes a form of community media. In some countries, puppets have been used to discuss taboo subjects that simply cannot be aired in

---

[4] http://www.crisinfo.org
[5] Topic Overview on Community Media, 19 January 2002 by Kevin Howley, *St James Encyclopedia of Popular Culture*, see http://www.findarticles.com

a less anonymous forum (Wanyeki 2000: 27). Similarly strong cases can be made for the use of audio towers, drama, audio-listening groups, cassettes and community blackboards.

There are many different forms of community media, or at least forms of community communications. 'A community ... creates, and is also created by, a community communication system,' argues Opubor (1999: 13). As a community's needs are diverse, this system requires different means of expression and different channels. These may well include what media professor Guy Berger would describe as 'folk media' such as rituals, dance and songs (Berger 1996: 2).[6] Indeed, in the pre-1990s period in South Africa, community media existed largely in the form of the alternative press but also in 'underground communications' such as graffiti, pamphlets and posters (Majozi 1999: 142).

For Berger, there are five types of media: state/public media; government media; corporate media; independent (commercial) media and community media. He suggests that one of the key distinctions lies between media institutions and groups whose core activity is something other than media output, such as churches (Berger 1996: 2).

The roots of contemporary definitions of community media in South Africa can be traced back to the deeply influential Jabulani! Freedom of the Airwaves conference held in the Netherlands in 1991. Though the conference was focused primarily on broadcast issues, its grappling with what constituted a community broadcaster was to have a significant impact on local policy initiatives, not least in the Independent IBA Act of 1993 which relied heavily on consensus reached at Jabulani!. The IBA Act developed a framework for the broadcast media environment in the new dispensation and included provision for the state broadcaster's change into a public broadcaster, the need for an independent regulator and the creation of a three tier broadcasting system comprising public, private and community broadcasting.

According to the Jabulani! resolutions, community or participatory broadcasting was 'initiated and controlled by members of a community, to express their concerns, needs and aspirations without outside interference' (Siemering 1997: 1). This idea of a media being for the community, by the community and through the community was to achieve popular currency in both popular and legal definitions of the sector.

But within this broad definition lay much that was, and remains, contested. How does one define ownership by the community, for instance, or spell out how 'by the community' translates into different forms of participation?

The Community Radio Manual (1999) attempts to spell out the ownership issue in more detail. It states that community participation is made up of three elements: the involvement of local residents in decision-making and participation in the work carried out at the community media organisation; the sharing of benefits accruing from ownership; and in the identification of needs with the aim of addressing them (Urgoiti 1999: 17). If each of these requirements is fulfilled, then the organisation can be defined as a community organisation.

The manual suggests that there is no fixed formula as each community is unique. The baseline requirement, in the case of radio, is that the station is owned, managed and

---

6 Conference paper, Community Voices Conference see http://www.journ.ru.ac.za

programmed by the community it serves. Similar classifications soon became applicable to print, audiovisual and multimedia operations.

The IBA Act also clarified the notion of community participation. It states that community participation is the active participation of a community in respect of attendance of meetings, involvement in fund-raising initiatives and directing the programming of the station through complaints or comments committees. It also noted a passive level of participation that includes donations to the organisation and, for example, dedications on air.

The Community Radio Manual states that, while there are many definitions for community media and though each organisation is unique and special, three definitive principles are now commonly accepted:
- Community media is owned, managed and programmed/filled by the people it serves.
- Community media are non-profit and respond to the community's expressed needs and priorities.
- Community media are accountable to community structures.

Berger has raised questions over the degree of community participation implied in the 'owned and controlled by the community' criterion. He argues it is unrealistic to expect continuous self-expression within a community and warns that participation can 'run out of steam' (Berger 1996: 4).[7] He adds that while community control is important, it can't be considered fundamental. The relationship between control and participation may also be more complex than it seems at first. What does community ownership mean? For Berger, the most important feature of community media is 'participation plus a progressive agenda' (4).

Even beyond a progressive agenda, some argue that community media must challenge the loci of contemporary political and social power. A Unesco work says: 'They present an alternative discourse from the communications agenda set by the dominant, socio-political or even cultural order' (Karikari 1999: 47). They should also contribute to the process of change. This is a common theme and has its roots in the origins of community media, and particularly community radio.

In the United States, where it first emerged, community radio began life as an anti-war platform challenging the political status quo. In South Africa too, the community media was 'instrumental in informing and mobilising communities against apartheid,' according to the Open Window Network's website.[8] In addition, the nascent sector functioned as a tool to counter state propaganda, and assisted in educating the masses about their rights to facilitate the building of strong community organisations.

There are those who argue the community media sector can only contribute significantly to democracy if it offers a counterpoint to prevailing voices and contemporary power. 'The community media agenda should start from the point of view of liberation from dominant power structures,' argues Berger (1996: 5). There is thus a strong view that a vital, even defining function of the community media should be the objective of political, preferably progressive, activism. But as well as resisting the forces of domination, some contend that community media has an additional function with regard to community unity

---

7 Conference paper, Community Voices Conference see http://www.journ.ru.ac.za
8 Website no longer live

and cohesion. According to the Caribbean media analyst Cholmondeley, community media enterprises 'can help to preserve and renew the glue that keeps communities together and become reliable sources of solutions that are shared with their communities and improve the quality of community decisions' (1999: 98).

There are demonstrably many characteristics used to capture the essence of what constitutes community media, including its non-commercial objectives and even its use of local or indigenous materials. The subject will be explored further below in this paper when the values that underpin the community media are considered in more detail. In the meantime, the National Community Media Forum (NCMF) suggests community media can be identified by five key features:

- It must be owned and controlled by the community, through its representatives.
- It must be non-profit.
- It must be accessible to the community it serves.
- The community must either be a geographic one or a community of interest.
- It must service disadvantaged communities.

And, while some of these key features are more commonly accepted than others, including the last one that is indeed ignored by the IBA Act but reinforced by broader policy guidelines, these five features can be presumed to be the current defining characteristics of the sector.

According to Chuck Scott: 'The process of controlling and producing communication is as important as the product itself. Both are seen as an integral part of the means towards enabling community access to, participation in and empowerment through creating and communicating their own messages to an audience of "common interest"' (1997: 3).

1.6.3 Why is community media important?

> Without a diversity of voices, democracy will be a mere swan-song.
> *Joel Netshitenzhe,*
> *CEO: GCIS*

This research paper has already alluded to the over-riding consensus that community media is a good, positive and even essential component for development and for democracy. This section provides the opinions of several local and international media analysts and policymakers who have voiced support for this belief.

Since the 1980s, Unesco has actively promoted the community media as an important agent for change and development. According to Opubor, 'Several reasons for funding community media as a social good have been advanced ... the bottom line of these suggestions is the need for communications and information policies, at the national level, which are sensitive to the plight of poorer communities, based on an understanding of the ways in which access to information can help them bridge the development gap and achieve better lives' (Opubor 1999: 22).

Wanyeki, who also contributed to the Unesco work, argues that while community media provides access to information, fosters debate, builds solidarity and allows for advocacy, 'in a broader sense, community media enables greater participation by communities in national and international affairs' (Wanyeki 1999: 30). For Fraser, 'community media can provide the platform for the public dialogue through which people can define who they are, what they want and how to get it, at the same time building long-term capacity to solve problems in ways that lead to sustainable social change and development' (2002: 70).

Several authors argue that a vital role of the community media sector is to make up for the increasingly globalised commercial media's incapacity to grapple with or to portray local issues and debates. 'The globalised commercial media can never respond to the socio-economic and development needs of the countries they reach, let alone those of marginalised communities within those countries' (Fraser 2002: 70). According to Karikari, another Unesco author, 'The existing media is not disposed to accommodate a different voice. Community media can also play a role in peace-building, socio-economic development, literacy and numeracy, urban social questions, cultural development (including linguistic), cultural creativity, democracy and good governance' (1999: 53).

The idea that the community media plays a role in social cohesion and identity building is a common theme. 'If you don't have a way to talk to yourselves, what have you got?' asks US analyst Cheryl Gibbs. She argues that the community media is the 'glue that holds a community together' (1995: 32). A community newspaper's biggest contribution to community life is – or should be – helping residents see what they have in common, not just where their differences lie, she writes.

The experience in the Caribbean region has been that the availability of responsive media in communities can reduce alienation and facilitate their integration into the larger society or region (Cholmondeley 1999: 114). The supply and access of media do appear to set parameters for democratic communication (Lundby 1997: 40).

In South Africa, sentiment concerning the role of the community media has been equally strong. The important Reconstruction and Development Programme (RDP) Base Document of 1994, one of the cornerstones of democratic policy in the post-apartheid era, declared that open debate and transparency in government and in society was considered crucial to both reconstruction and development. In its submission to the South African Human Rights Commission (SAHRC), the IBA stated that 'diversity, we believe, creates an environment in which different views can be exchanged and a respect for human rights can flourish' (11 February 2000: 1).[9]

Sue Valentine, a respected local commentator on community media issues, focuses on community radio which she believes is fundamentally different from both commercial and public service broadcasting: 'Community radio ... rests on the belief that the airwaves are a public resource. In the 'global village', access to the airwaves is vital to the basic human right to communicate. Community radio offers a forum in which ordinary people can exercise this fundamental right. It is the modern means by which ordinary people discuss their worlds – the village square of the twentieth century' (Valentine in Louw 1993: 71). Louw feels similarly that the community media 'is an essential aspect of building a strong civil society, one in which citizens are encouraged to express themselves and to exercise control over their own lives and environment' (1993: 71). The views of these few scholars and analysts are reflected in the resolutions and declarations of many multilateral organisations. The Non-Aligned Movement (NAM) stressed at its twelfth summit in Durban

---

9 http://www.iba.org.za/racism.html

in September 1998 that 'the establishment of a new world information and communications order aimed at ensuring impartiality and balance in the information flow, improving the information and communication infrastructure and capacity of development countries through the transfer of advanced information technology and expanding their access is more imperative than ever before' (NAM Report 1998: 2).

There are some countries, and even cases of democratic states, in which community media has not been assigned the same importance. In India, for instance, the community media does not exist largely due to government concerns over the espousal of separatist viewpoints and to prevent the publication or airing of radical political propaganda (Ninan, 2000: 31).

It is the understanding of the authors of this report, however, that the support, encouragement and flourishing of the community media sector is a vitally important goal in keeping with key national developmental, constitutional and democratic objectives.

Conclusion

Ultimately policymakers, regulators and enablers need to accept that a healthy media environment is one that is made up of all three tiers of media: public, private and community. Strategies need to be devised that enable each and every one of these tiers to develop and thrive in a spirit of co-operation. The very inception of the MDDA acknowledges that community media is here to stay. It has entered the mainstream. It has taken its rightful place on the media stage and will no longer be content with a demeaning, secondary role. This is the global trend. It is essential, given this understanding, that international examples of best practice are sought, that the level of the debate is raised and that modalities and strategies are framed that are relevant to our own experiences and priorities.

2 SMALL MEDIA AND THE POLICY ENVIRONMENT

2.1 Introduction

The policy environment in which South African small media organisations find themselves in 2004 is a complex one that touches on a broad range of legal, legislative, regulatory, political and even constitutional issues. This complexity is partly a reflection of the nature of the media itself and of the radical changes the sector is currently undergoing, and partly a reflection of the transforming society in which the media operates.

The media is a combination of too many elements to be easily categorised. It communicates, manufactures, prints, broadcasts, investigates, exposes, distributes, challenges, entertains, informs, to name but a few of its functions. In addition, the media has roles with regard to the consolidation of democracy, the promotion of development and diversity and the forging of a new, post-apartheid national identity. These are all difficult, contested processes that are tackled in different ways by different media.

While it is important to draw distinctions between the mainstream, commercial and community media sectors – as well as other types of community and development communications – much of the policy environment in which the various components of the media operate is shared. This overview will outline the broad policy environment as it affects the media in general but will also focus wherever possible on the specific needs and/or concerns of the small media sector and of its constituent parts.

In this chapter, we will look at a range of policy environments and examine how the small media in South Africa has located itself within them. The policy environment is essentially characterised by six standards that determine interaction and behaviour in the sector: the 1996 Constitution, Acts of Parliament, government policy directives, regulations issued by the regulatory authority, licence conditions, self-regulation and corporate regulations. Each of these will be considered in the overview below.

Prior to this, though, it is important to consider the values upon which the very nature of community media is based. It is these values that inform the policy pronouncements that govern and regulate the sector and that will have a significant impact on the future course of community media in South Africa.

2.2 Community media and values

> The freedom of people to express themselves is the most important of all rights that human beings claim in that it is only extinguished by death.
> *Raymond Louw*

A range of fundamental values underpin the existence and functioning of the community media in South Africa. They range from freedom of expression, diversity, pluralism, communication and transparency to accessibility, participation, independence and a not-for-profit financial positioning.

The expression of these values can be found in a variety of policy instruments ranging from multilateral organisation resolutions, such as the UN Declaration of Human Rights and domestic party manifestos to the 1996 Constitution. Some values are contained in less formal vehicles, for instance, in common practices or attitudes in the broader media sector. In many cases, these values have developed over time. Some continue to evolve while others are spelt out in legislation such as the IBA Act of 1993 or have been enshrined in the country's supreme law, the Constitution.

The 1996 Constitution sets out several vital principles that have a key impact on the functions, purpose and future of the community media sector. Perhaps pre-eminent is the right to the freedom of expression. According to American 'Founding Father' James Madison, freedom of expression is the only effectual guardian of every other right and, 'without it, tyranny can advance in silence' (Madison in Sparks 2003: 61).

Freedom of expression is enshrined in Section 16(1) of the 1996 Constitution which states: Everyone has the right to freedom of expression, which includes
a) freedom of the press and other media;
b) freedom to receive or impart information or ideas;
c) freedom of artistic creativity; and
d) academic freedom and freedom of scientific research.

The South African Constitutional Court has followed the lead of courts in many jurisdictions which have acknowledged that freedom of expression protects and fosters a number of values, including the pursuit of truth, the functioning of democracy and individual self-fulfilment (Maitland 2003).[10] These values lie at the very heart of the community media sector's role within our new, democratic society.

Van Eijk argues that in jurisprudence a distinction is made between so-called classical and social constitutional rights. He argues that freedom of expression is a classical right designed to protect citizens against the authorities. But freedom of expression is also, in current legal opinion, a social constitutional right. This means that apart from a passive task (non-interference), governments also have an active role to play in ensuring citizens are able to gain access to the media (1999: 236). The government, therefore, has a legal and arguably constitutional obligation to promote a media to which ordinary people can achieve access. It is arguable whether freedom of expression can be said to exist, for instance, in a situation where stark imbalances in access to media and communication exist and where marginalised groups have virtually no access to either.

The public's right to receive information of public interest and the media's role in providing that information is well recognised in international law (FXI 1996).[11] The gist of the many relevant declarations and conventions, quite a few of which are aimed at protecting minorities' rights, is the promotion of access to the media, cultural self-expression and tolerance. Freedom of expression is considered of central importance to each of these.

Other important lodestones of international law on the issue of freedom of expression include Article 5 of the International Convention on the Elimination of All Forms of Racial Discrimination (which requires states to guarantee the right of 'everyone without distinction ... the right to equal participation in cultural activities' and calls on governments to promote tolerance and broadmindedness) and the 1994 Committee of Ministers of the Council of Europe's Framework for the Protection of National Minorities,

---

10 http://www.maitlandco.com
11 http://www.fxi.org.za

SMALL MEDIA AND THE POLICY ENVIRONMENT

which states there shall be no discrimination in access to the media. These laws allow the possibility of creating and using groups' own media and to promote tolerance and cultural pluralism.

The 1996 Constitution also guarantees the right to equality, the equality of all languages, the multicultural nature of South Africa and the right to promote cultures, choice and diversity. Jane Duncan, community media activist, notes that there were significant differences between the way that freedom of expression was spelled out in the interim Constitution of 1993 and its final delineation in the 1996 Constitution (Duncan 2001: 26). One of the key differences concerns the treatment of hate speech. While unpopular and even offensive speech is protected by the 1996 Constitution, hate speech is not. This does not mean, however, that hate speech is banned, merely that it is not protected by the Constitution. This allows for a 'harms test' to be conducted to determine limitations on hate speech rather than a 'morality test' which would have been apposite to the Interim Constitution. This, argues Duncan, limits the potential for the abuse by people in power of a hate speech ban (Duncan 2003).[12]

The notions of equality and human dignity are also emphasised in the 1996 Constitution and both have relevance to media policy. A useful illustration of this was provided by the SAHRC's investigation into racism in the media in 1999. The commission received a complaint from the Black Lawyers Association and the Association of Black Accountants of South Africa that two newspapers (the *Sunday Times* and the *Mail & Guardian*) were racist in the way they reported on what was happening in South Africa, particularly where black people were the subjects of stories. The commission decided to expand its approach to examine racism in the media more broadly. Hearings were held in March 2000. In its submission to the commission, the IBA which later became Icasa argued that the Constitutional clauses on hate speech were 'sufficient protection against racism or sexism in all media' (IBA 2000). The IBA reminded the commission that independent regulatory bodies, including itself, existed to field any complaints in this regard.

Pluralism is another key aspect of the value matrix that lies at the root of the community media sector. It means the expression of as many different views as possible and is considered an essential element to the functioning of a healthy democracy. Giving 'voice to the voiceless' is a frequent refrain of community media activists. The need for a multiplicity of views, opinions as well as a variety of cultural, linguistic and religious expression, is supported by broad, democratic theory and is enshrined in a number of ways in the 1996 Constitution. There are, however, different ways of ordering pluralism: internally, in which one licence is awarded per area and other media are ensured access, and externally, in which several licences are awarded in one area and the media compete (Van Eijk 1992: 238).

The European Court of Human Rights upheld pluralism and the right to freedom of expression as key values in a judgment in 1993. Other declarations can be found in the International Covenant on Civil and Political Rights (which also urges equal access to the media for all groups, including minorities), Article 2 of the African Charter on Human and People's Rights and in the 1993 UN Declaration on the Rights of Persons Belonging to National, Ethnic, Religious and Linguistic Minorities. This latter declaration obliges states

---

12 http://www.fxi.org.za

to 'take measures to enable persons belonging to minorities to express their characteristics and to develop their culture, language, religion, traditions and customs' (FXI 1996).[13]

There is a close correlation between pluralism and diversity, which is considered in more detail below.

Transparency is a value which has its origins in French law but that obviously has applicability and relevance in the South African context. Transparency has a direct correlation to pluralism. Transparency literally means the ability to see through a structure or process. In social terms, transparency means a common understanding of the functioning of organisations and of the means by which decisions are made and resources allocated. With regard to the media, transparency also applies to the ownership and control of a media organisation: 'It must be clear who has authority over a medium: if it is known who controls it, it can be ascertained which pluralistic function is threatened' (Van Eijk 1992: 238).

In the 1960s, a new form of democracy became prominent: participatory democracy. The form implied more co-determination in matters that were relevant to those involved, and more participation in the formation and expression of opinions by those directly concerned (Jankowski et al. 1992). The shift led to the rise in significance of political issues at a local level, such as the environment and housing, which in turn accelerated the need for and growth of community media. It was a media in which the principle of participation was a central dimension, just as it was to the new form of democracy from which it emanated.

Participation came to be a valued aspect not only of the organisation of community media structures but also of the content produced. The genesis of community television, for instance, arose in Canada in the 1960s with the Fogo Island Project. For the first time, the project encouraged the subjects of television documentaries to take part in the production process creating a unique collaborative relationship between filmmakers and subjects. 'The use of participatory media practices to enhance community communication, to spur and support local government initiatives and to promote a sense of common purpose and identity has become the hallmark of community media organisations around the world' (Howley 2003).[14]

The importance of participation gained new impetus when it was realised how critical the notion was to development. By the 1990s, the principle that deemed participation to be a requisite for successful development had gained primacy. An African Charter for Popular Participation in Development and Transformation was signed in 1990 (Wanyeki 2000: 25). The importance of community participation is highlighted in a range of contemporary South African policy initiatives including the Integrated Sustainable Rural Development Strategy (ISRDS), the URP and IDP. The community media sector not only facilitates such participation between communities and government but embodies it too in the ownership, management and output of its organisations.

Just as participation's role in successful development came to form the consensual position, so too did communication undergo a conceptual transformation. In 1976, Unesco issued a statement in which it re-defined communication and its role in

---

13 http://www.fxi.org.za
14 Topic Overview on Community Media, 19 January 2002 by Kevin Howley, *St James Encyclopedia of Popular Culture*, see http://www.findarticles.com

SMALL MEDIA AND THE POLICY ENVIRONMENT

development. The report said: 'In the past, the role of communication in human society was seen essentially as a method to inform and influence people. It is now being proposed that communication should be understood as a process of social interaction through a balanced exchange of information and experience ... This shift in perception implies the predominance of dialogue over monologue. The aim is to achieve a system of horizontal communication based upon an equitable distribution of resources and facilities enabling all persons to send as well as receive messages' (Prehn 1992: 258).

Communications for development came to imply two-way communications rather than the top-down approach used previously. Two forms of community media developed out of this: independent, privately-owned organisations with a community development orientation which were produced with some level of community participation; and communications initiatives in the development industry which sought to incorporate community participation in ownership, management and production. 'The nature of community media is participatory and the purpose ... is development, a process of public and private dialogue through which people define who they are, what they want and how they can get it' (Wanyeki 2000: 31).

A crucial element of communications is the distinction it makes in the role of the consumer or participant and in the 'two-way' flow of information and dialogue. In a discussion document of the CMS Task Team (CMSTT) to the Minister of Communications, two-way information flow, appropriate technology, redress and diversity were all stressed as vital elements of the community media. The task team pointed out that community media 'is aimed at transferring people from being passive consumers of media to being active participants in telling their own stories, communicating their needs and accessing information that is relevant to their lives' (CMSTT 2003: 3).

The issue of non-profit is an extremely common principle underpinning the community media sector and its development. It is also a contentious element. The general (global) understanding is that commercialism endangers the function and independence of community media, making it dependent on the demands of advertisers. It is often not possible for community media organisations to avoid the pressures of commercialisation altogether but this process needs to be conducted with great care. As community media commentator Donald R. Browne has argued: 'Every source of income brings with it some potential liabilities, usually of control or dependence' (Browne 1996: 221). A US based community television producer, Jesikah Maria Ross, has pointed out that there are few, if any, cases where commercial considerations have not impacted negatively on community television's production and programming commitments to disadvantaged, minority or counter-cultural groups (Ross in Duncan & Seleoane 1998).

In a 2000 Unesco report, non-profit is clearly presented as a feature of community media. The sector 'is broadly defined as non-governmental and non-corporate ... Ideally, community media should be produced, managed and owned by, for and about the community they serve, which can either be a geographic community or a community of interest' (Wanyeki 2000: 29). The value of working without a profit motive is also a value that was to be ingrained in global concepts of community media. The requirement that community media organisations must be non-profit falls into the IBA Act of 1993 and into most South African definitions of the community media.

THE PEOPLE'S VOICE

An anti-establishment attitude was a frequent attribute of early community media organisations in the US, Europe and in South Africa too. Examples were the anti-war activism of the very first community radio station in America (Pacifica Radio Network) and the pirate radio stations (Radio Caroline, Radio Mercy) that sprung up in Europe in the 1950s and 1960s. Lew Hill, who established Pacifica, was a journalist and conscientious objector who was disillusioned with the state of American broadcasting at the time. The community radio sector that sprung up particularly in the US in the post-war years came to represent an 'indispensable alternative' to the anti-Communist hysteria of the 1950s. Political resistance and activism was also a feature of community radio in Italy, France and in many countries of Western Europe where trade unions, leftist parties and movements used the medium to oppose the prevailing political authority. It was also a notable feature of the anti-apartheid alternative print media, who were the forbears of the community media movement in South Africa. Many, including journalism academic Professor Guy Berger, consider resistance and activism to be definitive values of the sector.

This anti-establishment attitude naturally provokes criticism from those who argue that the community media's principal function is to be a vehicle for development communications. Governments, in particular, have attempted both in South Africa and abroad to harness community media organisations to function as formal communications channels. Community media activists warn, however, that allowing media organisations to become government communication outlets threatens the other key values of independence, diversity and freedom of expression.

An important site of community media values is the IBA Act, which includes a number of different notions including access, diversity and equality. These are commonly agreed in international broadcasting. The Act defines access as the availability of (broadcasting) services to all citizens (universal access) and includes the right of citizens to reliable, accurate and timely information to participate meaningfully in society.

The development of community media also receives support from the notion of creating access to the means of media production. Both the Green Paper on Broadcast Policy and a Technical Task Team's discussion document on broadcasting emphasise that 'access is a critical area that needs urgent address through appropriate policy intervention' (TTT: 10).[15]

Diversity is presented in the legislation as the availability of a variety of choices of information, education and entertainment in a range of linguistic, cultural, religious and regional programming. The five dimensions of diversity listed in the Act are:
- Diversity of media functions (information, education and entertainment);
- Diversity of content (programming);
- Diversity of representation of different groups and peoples in society;
- Diversity of geography or locale; and
- Diversity of ownership.

Equality in the Act is understood to mean proportionality and fairness when it comes to different groups' access and representation within the media. The principle is important when it comes to promoting change and correcting imbalances. It encourages new entrants, the sharing of cultural goods (and therefore nation-building) and the application of fair employment practices including employment equity.

---

15 http://www.icasa.org.za

SMALL MEDIA AND THE POLICY ENVIRONMENT

Diversity of opinion is directly related to independence, editorial freedom, the limitation of advertisers' influence on content, the existence and application of a code of conduct as well as a complaints mechanism. Independence is naturally a vital component of the community media sector's functioning. It is a value that has a direct bearing on pluralism, diversity and freedom of expression.

The notions of unity and even nation-building are also encapsulated within the legislation. The law urges community media organisations to safeguard, enrich and strengthen the cultural, political, social and economic fabric of South Africa. The community media sector's power to enhance unity and identity in positive ways has been repeatedly stressed both in South Africa and internationally.

As with so many aspects of community media, and reflective of the sector's changeable and complex nature, there are some values that do not form part of the international consensus but which are nonetheless important in the South African context. In a speech to the Freedom of Expression Institute-National Community Media Forum on 14 July 1999, GCIS CEO Joel Netshitenzhe listed several principles that he believed underpinned the functioning and role of the community media sector in South Africa. These are worth stating, and are listed as follows:

- Partnership: a consultative spirit is necessary between government, civil society and the people;
- An enabling environment is necessary as a catalyst for transformation;
- The monopoly of the means of discourse must be broken. To achieve this, the media industry, government and community media organisations will need to look beyond self-interest;
- Change in the media environment must be meaningful. This means issues of ownership, newsroom composition, distribution and printing need to be included in the process;
- The sector needs to avoid pitfalls like arrogance and laziness and search for a coincidence of interest;
- Further debate. The MDDA cannot be the be-all and end-all of policy debate but must be part of a bigger process of transformation addressing all elements of the media;
- The market will not, by itself, resolve issues of transformation within the media;
- South Africa must learn from international experience;
- Support and acknowledgement needs to be mobilised for other networks which provide information to communities, such as folklore. This begs the question: what is media?;
- Reinforcing social solidarity; and
- Providing a universal service.

Finally, the community media sector will inevitably be affected by the values that underpin the national political agenda. We have already spoken of the Constitutional values that are represented with both national politics and the community media. But, in addition to this, there is pressure for community media organisations to conform to corollary national objectives, such as '*Batho Pele*' (People First) and poverty alleviation. These 'values' will be dealt with in the following section.

With the broad values now in place, let us consider the development of actual policy with regard to the media in general and community media in particular.

THE PEOPLE'S VOICE

2.3 Overview of policy developments prior to 1994

The formation of media policy in South Africa began in earnest in 1990. It was at this time that a series of conferences, debates and even protest actions gave significant impetus to policy matters and focused attention on the importance of the media sector and its role in the transition to democracy, and beyond. Of course there were many laws and even policy to do with the media in South Africa prior to 1990, not least the 120 laws that the apartheid government put in place over decades to restrict the media and limit freedom of expression and association. There were also moments in the period pre-1990 when media issues reached the public domain, such as former State President P W Botha's infamous late night telephone calls to the South African Broadcasting Corporation (SABC) with instructions to recast the news.

This chapter will, however, not dwell on apartheid media restrictions nor on the policy that articulated these attitudes. Instead, we will focus on progressive media policy and on the extraction of principles and policies that inform the current way of thinking.

It is worth alluding briefly to the ideological debates that surround the existence and encouragement, in policy terms, of the community media. This branch of the media draws support from decentralisation theory, which is a branch of the modernisation model (Tleane 2002: 3). The theory, as espoused by eminent thinkers such as Paulo Freire, advocates a localisation agenda in several spheres of social development. Scholars have supported and opposed decentralisation theory. Critics suggest it advances the agenda of neo-liberals by disengaging development from the state, while advocates argue it has the potential to give communities a voice and, in South Africa, serve the needs of previously disadvantaged communities (Tleane 2002: 4).

But before the watershed moment of the early 1990s, there were a few, important prior developments that came to inform progressive media policy in South Africa. They not only steep media policy in the history of the progressive political movements but also provide pointers for the future.

The Atlantic Charter signed on 14 August 1941 by Franklin D Roosevelt and Winston Churchill was intended to be a declaration of what it was the free world was fighting for when it took on the Nazis and their allies in World War II. In declaring that the two democratic superpowers of the time wished 'to see sovereign rights and self-government restored to those who have been forcibly deprived of them,' the Atlantic Charter gave great hope and inspiration to African political leaders. In the wake of the Atlantic Charter, the African National Congress (ANC) adopted a response to the Atlantic Charter (usually called the African Claims' Document) in December 1943 which called for full citizenship for all South Africans as well as 'full participation in the educational, political and economic activities' of the state.[16] Attached to the African Claims document was a Bill of Rights that declared the 'Freedom of the Press' as a fundamental right. In 1946, the scope of freedoms was extended a little further when the UN General Assembly passed a resolution 59(1) of 1946 that declared that freedom of information was a fundamental human right.

Not long after the African Claims document was adopted and in the wake of World War II, one of the most important multinational pronouncements of human history was made with the UN Universal Declaration of Human Rights, which was unveiled on 10 December 1949.

---

16 See 'African Claims in South Africa' document http://www.anc.org.za/ancdocs/history/claims.html

SMALL MEDIA AND THE POLICY ENVIRONMENT

Article 19 has become a landmark of media policy. The article reads as follows: 'Everyone has the right to freedom of opinion and expression; this right includes the freedom to hold opinions without interference and to seek, receive and impart information and ideas through any media regardless of frontiers.' The article has been a lodestone for media activists ever since and continues to influence constitutional law and media policy both in South Africa and across the world.

The sentiments of Article 19 were adopted and expanded upon a few years later when South Africans came together to launch the Freedom Charter at Kliptown in 1955. The Charter did not mention the media specifically but did declare that South Africa would one day be governed by a law that would 'guarantee to all their right to speak, to organise to meet together, to publish, to preach, to worship and to educate their children'. It also called for the 'free exchange of books and ideas', the right of all people to use their own languages and to develop their own folk culture and customs. These are all rights and guarantees that clearly set the tone for future media policy and which emphasise the need and importance of communities' access to media.

Though the years between the launching of the Freedom Charter in the mid-1950s and the late 1980s were important years for the development of community media in other parts of the world, media policy during this time in South Africa was about censorship and repression rather than diversity and accessibility. For almost three decades, little media policy of note emerged.

By the end of the 1980s, however, things had begun to change. In 1989, the Congress of South African Trade Unions (Cosatu) set up a national consultative process concerning media policy that 'crystallised a rudimentary network of left-wingers interested in media policy work' (Louw 1993: 9). Sadly, the initiative floundered in the face of more pressing national priorities, but a seed had been planted. The increasing impetus of political negotiations at home reflected the rapid advances media policy was making abroad. Central to this was the growing belief that being able to communicate and the receiving and transmitting of information (rather than just the right to information) were as important to democracy and development as other more traditional human rights.

Unesco adopted a resolution on 'Communication in the service of humanity' in 1989. The resolution called for the free flow of ideas by word and image; the promotion of a wider and better balanced dissemination of information without any obstacle to freedom of expression; and, the development of all appropriate means of strengthening communities in order to increase their participation in the communications process. Only a year later, the spirit of the Unesco resolution was adopted by the full UN General Assembly. In the UN resolution adopted on 11 December 1990, all countries were asked to:

> co-operate and interact with a view to reducing existing disparities in the information flow at all levels by increasing assistance for the development of communication infrastructures and capabilities in developing countries, with due regard for their needs and the priorities attached to such areas by those countries, and in order to enable them and the public, private or other media in developing countries to develop their own information and communication policies freely and independently and increase their participation of media and individuals in the communication process, and to ensure a free flow of information at all levels.

Back at home, a system to provide subsidies to non-commercial media was mooted in various quarters in the 1980s and emerged in a 1989 Durban Media Trainers Group discussion document. The paper, which was spelt out in greater detail at a Rhodes University Policy Workshop in September 1990, placed the prospect firmly on the mass democratic movement's table. The idea was that a state-created fund would be established to ensure media diversity and would be funded in part by taxing the existing commercial media. The idea led, by 1992, to the establishment of the Independent Media Diversity Trust (IMDT) which was intended to source and channel funding to the then struggling alternative press. The IMDT failed a few years later when its own funding dried up. The alternative media, other than the *Mail & Guardian*, also collapsed in the early 1990s. *New Nation*, *Vrye Weekblad*, the *New African* and *South* all ceased operations in this period.

On 25 August 1990, 2 000 people marched on the SABC offices in Auckland Park, Johannesburg. The demonstration was a watershed moment in the evolution of domestic media policy. It marked the galvanisation of progressive media workers to resist the top-down reform of broadcasting anticipated by a National Party (NP) government in its dying days. The march was principally a protest against the appointment of the Viljoen Task Group, a body headed by H C Viljoen, then chairman of the SABC, intended to investigate the future of broadcasting in South and southern Africa. The protest was led by the Campaign for Open Media (COM) which was established jointly by the Film and Allied Workers Organisation (FAWO) and Cosatu's anti-privatisation committee.

As the task group proceeded with its work, the ANC issued a statement setting out its views on the democratisation of the airwaves: 'The ANC stands for the genuine freedom of the airwaves which will create space for public, commercial and community broadcasting to flourish to the maximum in a dynamic and diverse broadcasting environment' (ANC statement, 29 October 1991). As it turned out, even the ANC conceded that the Viljoen task group made some useful recommendations, including the establishment of an independent regulatory body, the framing of a new broadcasting Act, the devolution of political control from the public broadcaster and the improvement of the accessibility of the broadcast medium. But the ANC statement clearly shows how the notion of community media was beginning to infiltrate formal policy processes.

A series of influential conferences in the early 1990s brought in international experience and gave substance to early outlines of progressive media policy. Most important were the 'Jabulani! Freedom of the Airwaves' Conference of August 1991 and the University of Boputhatswana media policy workshop of September 1991. At the Jabulani conference, community broadcasting was defined as 'initiated and controlled by members of a community of interest, or a geographical community, to express their concerns, needs and aspirations without outside interference and subject to the regulations of an independent regulatory body' (Louw 1993: 307).

Also important was the Patriotic Front conference in Durban in October 1991 and the ANC Department of Information and Publicity seminar in November 1991, at which the ANC circulated its draft Media Charter. The document drew heavily on earlier conference debates and highlighted issues like the equitable distribution of media resources, diversity, access, skills, ownership and affirmative action. Agreement on the Charter, described by Louw as a 'crucial turning point within the ANC's approach to the media',

SMALL MEDIA AND THE POLICY ENVIRONMENT

was adopted by the party's top decision-making body, the National Executive Committee, on 13 January 1992 (Teer-Tomaselli in Louw 1993: 231).

The ANC Media Charter, which was a 'deliberately Utopian, statement of intent', included a clause stating: 'All communities shall have access to the skills required to receive and disseminate information' (Teer-Tomaselli in Louw, 1993: 231). While the main preoccupation of the seminar was what to do with the SABC and how to minimise its pro-NP impact in the looming first democratic election, it also emphasised several aspects. These included repeated endorsements for the idea of media as a vehicle for empowerment and for the value of the media in terms of education, training and development (1993: 237).

Discussions in South Africa were certainly informed by happenings not only elsewhere in the world but elsewhere in Africa. In 1991, a statement of principles was drawn up by African journalists calling for a free, independent and pluralistic media on the continent and throughout the world. The Windhoek Declaration was to become a benchmark for the UN and for all organisations in the media field. In its preamble, the declaration noted that its lineage included Article 19 of the Universal Declaration of Human Rights and UN General Assembly Resolution 59(1) of 1946 (which declared that freedom of information is a fundamental human right) as well as Unesco's Resolution on the free flow of ideas of 1989.

The Windhoek Declaration, which focused specifically on print media, included these important policy statements:
- The establishment, maintenance and fostering of an independent, pluralistic and free press is essential to the development and maintenance of democracy in a nation and for economic development.
- An independent press means independence from governments, politicians, economic control or from the control of materials or infrastructure essential for the dissemination of newspapers, magazines and periodicals.
- A pluralistic press means the end of monopolies of any kind and the existence of the greatest possible number of outlets reflecting the widest possible range of opinion.
- Direct funding is a priority to ensure the development and establishment of non-government publications that reflect society as a whole.
- All funding should aim to encourage pluralism as well as independence.

Meanwhile, the SABC had proceeded with a commercialisation process of its operations during 1991, prompting the launch of a Campaign for Independent Broadcasting (CIB) that was launched on 14 November 1992. The campaign was aimed at halting the unilateral restructuring of broadcasting. Previous efforts had been made to reform the SABC. In 1987, the then minister responsible for broadcasting, Alwyn Schlebusch, had established a task group on broadcasting in South and southern Africa. The report of the Schlebusch task group, however, was never published. It was in any case concerned primarily with the regulation of broadcasting in the former Transkei, Bophuthatswana, Venda and Ciskei (TBVC) 'homeland' states.

The Viljoen task group's findings were made public in spite of the protests and opposition. The task group's recommendations included the reduction of the SABC's dependency on advertising, the removal of signal distribution duties from the SABC and the encouragement of local programme content.

2.4 Overview of policy developments: post-1994

In its discussion document published in March 1998, the Technical Task Team on Broadcasting Policy (TTT) declared that 'large sections of the population have no choice of services and sometimes receive no services at all. A majority of South Africans rely on a single service, usually radio, to meet their vast broadcasting needs. In rural areas, a single radio station or a single TV service might, at best, define the choice of services'. The document noted that of South Africa's 11 official languages 'clearly many are not adequately served' (TTT 1998: 1).

It has not been to the small media's benefit that its complexity has seen it fall under the ambit of several government departments from communications and arts, culture, science and technology to trade and industry as well as telecommunications. It has been argued that squabbling between departments over who is to take the leadership role has already caused significant damage to the effective roll-out of ICT in South Africa (Benjamin 2001: 99–104).

It is perhaps a consequence of convergence that more and more government departments are becoming involved in the platforms community media themselves hope to use, as multi-departmental community centres are established and as access to media skills and technology becomes part of different departments' strategies. A DoC plan places community radio at the interface between rural communities and the Internet while small, medium and micro enterprises (SMMEs), traditionally a responsibility of the Department of Trade and Industry (DTI) are now eligible for multimedia licences from Icasa if they operate in under-serviced areas.

We have already alluded to the complexity of the media's functions and the multifaceted nature of its interconnections with society. Here we look at some of the legislation and policy that has emanated out of government since 1994 and which has had an impact on the workings of the community media sector and its place within the social and political framework.

From its earliest days, small media was understood to have important and positive developmental consequences for its participants and audiences. As a component, conduit and even catalyst for development, it is necessary for the small media sector to acknowledge and dovetail with government policy aimed at bolstering development. This, naturally, needs to happen while bearing in mind principles mentioned earlier, including editorial integrity and independence. This policy has taken many forms emanating out of several ministries.

2.4.1 Legislation relevant to the small media sector

The following pieces of legislation are among the most important:

The Independent Broadcasting Authority Act (1993): Though certain aspects of this legislation, including the council itself, have been stripped out and built into other laws, the basic framework of the Act remains in place. Requirements placed on radio and television licence holders are set out as well as the procedures for applications.

The Labour Relations Act (1995): The Act has application to the community media sector as it promotes employee participation in decision-making, facilitates collective bargaining

SMALL MEDIA AND THE POLICY ENVIRONMENT

at the workplace and at sectoral level, regulates the right to strike and provides for the resolution of labour disputes through statutory conciliation, mediation and arbitration. This report suggests that at least 5 000 people are linked directly to the sector.

The Telecommunications Act (1996): The key elements of this legislation were absorbed into the Icasa Act (see below). The Telecommunications Act was designed to regulate telecommunications activities and control the radio frequency spectrum. The legislation set up the SATRA, which was tasked with regulating radio frequencies, apparatus and the control of radio activities. It also entrenches the idea of universal service in law, and creates a digital backbone to build an Internet economy.

The Films and Publications Act (1996): This Act overturned notorious legislation of the same name passed in 1974. The 1996 Act sets up a structure through which any publications or films that are intended for distribution or exhibition are required to pass. Films and publications are classified by a board, age restrictions can be imposed and consumer advice is given. Distribution of any prohibited film or publication is a criminal offence in terms of the legislation. The general attitude, however, is much less restrictive than in the past and a broad principle is applied which seeks to minimise harm.

The Lotteries Act (1997): The Act provides for payment of lottery monies for projects that promote the arts, culture and national historical or cultural heritage. The Act also governs the holding of promotional competitions and sets a number of regulations in this regard. These include that the competition may not be too similar to the national lottery and also that participating in promoting competitions should not be the only or even the substantial inducement to a person to purchase or use the goods or services to which the competition relates.

The Competition Act (1998): Makes provisions concerning monopolistic behaviour, price collusion and access to general services. A Commission established by the Act ensures prohibition of anti-competitive agreements and/or abuse of a dominant position. The Commission also considers applications for approval of mergers. The Competition Commission, set up by the Act, has not yet investigated the electronic media. This is because of a memorandum of understanding between the Commission and Icasa that sets out the relationship and provides for how issues of potential dual jurisdiction will be handled. Competition issues concerning broadcasting thus falls under Icasa.

The Employment Equity Act (1998): The legislation is aimed at achieving a diverse workforce that is broadly representative of the South African population. Companies are required to draw up employment equity plans and file these with government.

The White Paper on Broadcast Policy (1998): Developed by the DoC, the White Paper was a precursor to the Broadcasting Act and had the following as its underlying principles:
- Access for all;
- Diversity is a framework of national unity;
- Free expression;
- Democratising the airwaves;
- Nation-building; and
- Special emphasis on educational broadcasting.

The people's voice

The White Paper noted the growth of community radio and said a national strategy was needed to encourage community radio in rural and other needy areas. The White Paper also sets out the priorities of community radio and outlines a community broadcasting service mandate. Government commits itself in the White Paper to 'act as a catalyst' to help community broadcasting fulfil its mission.

The Postal Services Act (1998): This Act was promulgated in 2000 and provides for the appointment of a postal regulator. The Act was amended in 2001 to make fresh provision for the composition of the Postal Regulator, regulate postal services and for the operational functions of the postal company, including its universal service obligations.

The Skills Development Act (1998): This Act provides an institutional framework to devise and implement national, sector and workplace strategies to develop and improve the skills of the South African workforce; to integrate those strategies within the NQF contemplated in the South African Qualifications Authority Act, 1995; to provide for learnerships that lead to recognised occupational qualifications; and to provide for the financing of skills development by means of a levy-financing scheme and a National Skills Fund.

The Broadcasting Act (1999): The Act supplied guidelines for the broadcasting system as a whole but made specific provision for community radio. The Act defines a community broadcasting service the same way as in the IBA Act. It also added:
- A community broadcasting service should be controlled by a democratically-elected board representative of all sectors of communities in the licenced service area.
- Community radio programming must reflect the needs of all people in communities served, including cultural, religious and demographic.

The Broadcasting Act also states that community radio programming must emphasise community issues not normally dealt with by other broadcasting services and should be informative, educational and entertaining; should highlight grassroots community issues; should promote democratic values and should improve the quality of peoples' lives. It indicates that where profits are made by community radio organisations, these should be invested for the benefit of the community. The Act tasks the IBA to hold a public investigation to determine priorities within the community radio sector as well as a similar process to investigate community television especially with regard to ownership and control. It also calls for an investigation into the viability and impact of community television.

The Independent Communications Authority of South Africa Act (2000): The Icasa Act replaced the IBA and SATRA and amended substantive parts of the Telecommunications Act of 1996, the IBA Act of 1993 and the Broadcasting Act of 1999. The Icasa Act combined the functions of the IBA and SATRA into one, independent, regulatory authority, Icasa. Icasa has already indicated that it considers Section 50 of the IBA Act (which sets out cross-media ownership limitations) as unworkable as it confuses readership with circulation. Icasa has now pronounced on this in their proposed amendments to the legislation as a result of an inquiry into commercial radio.

The Municipal Systems Act (2000): The Act sets out the formal definition of community participation as well as the procedures associated with IDPs. It includes the provision that municipalities must communicate relevant information to their communities including the rights and duties of a community in the language preferred and used within a

municipality. The Act states that when anything must be notified by a municipality through the media to the local community in terms of this Act or any other applicable legislation, it must be done:
(a) In the local newspaper or newspapers of its area;
(b) In a newspaper or newspapers circulating in its area and determined by the council as a newspaper of record; or
(c) By means of radio broadcasts covering the area of the municipality.

The Act also provides a regulatory framework for municipal service partnerships, particularly processes such as competitive bidding, dealing with unsolicited proposals, and contract monitoring and compliance, which gives legal effect to the framework agreement on restructuring municipal services signed between government and Cosatu on 16 December 1998.

The Open Democracy Bill (1998): This seeks to implement Section 32 of the Constitution by giving all citizens access to state information, subject to certain restrictions. The Bill was split into three for legislative purposes. The three Acts derived from the Bill are:
- *Promotion of Access to Information Act* (2000): This Act gives effect to the enshrined access to information clause in the Constitution (Section 32(1)). It allows access to information held by public bodies or other persons or bodies which is required for the exercise or protection of rights. The rules are different, depending on whether a media organisation requires information from a public or a private body. If it is public, procedural requirements need to be fulfilled. There are several grounds on which a public body can refuse to provide the information. They include:
  - If it entails giving personal information about a third party;
  - If it endangers the safety of an individual;
  - If the records are legally privileged;
  - If it relates to defence, security, international relations, economic or financial welfare of South Africa; and
  - If it is a vexatious or frivolous request.

  A private body may refuse to supply requested information on a number of grounds including privacy, safety or confidentiality. Applications for information that are in the public interest override grounds for refusal of both private and public bodies. The overall intention of the Act is to provide for 'a more open and trusting society'.
- *Protected Disclosures Act* (2000): This Act protects whistleblowers either within government or the private sector and prevents them from losing their jobs or benefits after disclosing corrupt behaviour or acts within their organisation.
- *Promotion of Administrative Justice Act* (2000): This Act gives effect to the right to administrative action that is lawful, reasonable and procedurally fair and to the right to written reasons for administrative action. One of the purposes of the Act is to create a culture of accountability, openness and transparency in the public administration or in the exercise of a public power.

The Telecommunications Amendment Act (2001): Creates provision for the awarding of multimedia licences and defines the concept. The Act also regulates mobile cellular telecommunication services.

The Broadcasting Amendment Act (2002): Calls for the creation of two regional television stations for South Africa. The Act, which amends the IBA Act of 1993 and the Icasa Act of

2000, also converts the SABC into a public company and makes provision for the application and granting of television licences.

The Regulation of Interception of Communications and Provision of Communication-related Information Act (2002): The Act, as amended, prohibits the unauthorised interception and monitoring of communications. It also provides for the establishment of interception centres, prohibits the manufacturing or sale of certain equipment and establishes an Internet Service Providers Assistance Fund.

The Media Development and Diversity Agency Act (2002): This Act establishes the MDDA.

The Electronic Communications and Transaction Act (2002): The Act provides for the development of a national e-strategy, promotes universal access to electronic communications and transactions and prevents the abuse of information systems. The national e-strategy is required to include programmes and means to achieve universal access, human resource development and development of SMMEs. The strategy is also required to set out existing government initiatives directly or indirectly relevant to or impacting on the national e-strategy and, if applicable, how such initiatives are to be utilised in attaining the objectives of the national e-strategy. This law also seeks to make government services accessible online, promotes universal and affordable access to electronic communications and transactions, promotes adoption and optimal use of electronic communications and transaction by the historically disadvantaged, encourages 'e-health' and 'e-learning'; and provides more protection for consumers. The Act sets out principles for the protection of personal information data, the principles of electronic collection of data and the management and protection of critical databases as well as restrictions on the disclosure of information.

The Convergence Bill (2003): The acknowledgement of the process of convergence of personal telecommunications with broadcasting has resulted in this draft legislation.

2.4.2 Administrative steps relevant to the small media sector

In 1994, the SABC Board was restructured and the IBA launched a 'Triple Enquiry into the Protection and Viability of the Public Broadcaster, cross-media control, Local Content and South African Music'. The inquiry represented the IBA's first important step toward the restructuring of the domestic broadcasting system.

A critical moment in the development of policy around information, communication and the media arose in 1996 with the Task Group on Government Communication (Comtask). Among Comtask's many important recommendations were:
- The creation of the GCIS;
- The acknowledgement of MPCCs as a key objective of government policy;
- A lack of media diversity results in an information bottleneck;
- The ownership and control of distribution and printing infrastructure are critical areas that need to be addressed to promote media diversity; and
- Proposes the establishment of the MDDA.

As a result of Comtask, a National Communication and Information System (NCIS), which is co-ordinated by the GCIS, was established. The system is intended to provide

SMALL MEDIA AND THE POLICY ENVIRONMENT

development communication and information to the public with the purpose of ensuring they become active participants in changing their lives for the better.

The main responsibility of the GCIS itself, which was to play a crucial role in the community media sector, is to keep the public informed about all the issues that affect their daily lives. The GCIS also aims to:
- Provide all South Africans with information on their rights and how to access them;
- Inform people on how they can use the prevailing socio-economic conditions to improve their personal circumstances and help to build a better South Africa for all; and
- Use community radio stations to reach the masses of illiterate people, mostly in the rural areas, and to focus particularly on those who were marginalised in the past and deprived of their rights.

A Government Communication Planning Forum (GCPF) has been set up to ensure co-operation between GCIS and the directorates of communications in various other government departments.

Around the same time, in 1996, the IBA launched its Triple Enquiry into the Protection and Viability of the Public Broadcaster, Cross-Media Control, Local Content and South African Music. A number of important regulations in each of these areas were forthcoming as a consequence of the Triple Enquiry and are now enshrined principally in the Icasa Act of 2000.

In 1998, various stakeholders (including Print Media South Africa [PMSA], NCMF and the IMDT) got together to look at ways in which media diversity in South Africa could be fostered. A print development agency was mooted to provide various forms of assistance to existing and emerging small print media to encourage their development. By the end of 1999, however, the process had broken down due to a lack of consensus. In 2000, the PDU was established, but as an internal division of PMSA.

On 29 November 2000, the GCIS launched a draft paper on Media Development and Diversity. The MDDA had been proposed by the Comtask report of 1996 as an independent, statutory body funded by government, the media industry and donors with the purpose of assisting the development of community media and promoting media diversity. The GCIS pointed to a number of policy predecessors for the establishment of the MDDA including the National Action Plan for the Promotion and Protection of Human Rights, which was published in 1998 and which emphasised freedom of expression and media diversity, as well as the Bill of Rights in the Constitution.

According to the policy draft, the MDDA would operate on the best principles of corporate governance and would use as its principal funding criteria: good governance, contributions to media development and diversity, community representation and participation. The GCIS noted the failure of the IMDT in 1998 and argued that media diversity schemes had been state-assisted even in Europe since the 1950s on the basis that market forces alone would not achieve sufficient diversity.

In 2001, the Media Institute of Southern Africa (MISA) noted that the southern African region 'lacks policies for the promotion of comprehensive, in-depth and impartial news and information coverage – particularly at the local level. What is required is a media environment that ensures access to minorities and provides culturally relevant information in local languages.'

It was also in 2001 that the Windhoek Declaration was extended to the broadcast sector with the unveiling of an African Charter of Broadcasting. This Charter noted that freedom of expression included the right to communicate and access to the means of communication. It called for the equal allocation of frequencies between the public service, commercial broadcasters and the community sector. It also noted ruefully that since the Windhoek Declaration, 'little of a practical nature was undertaken to promote the community, rural or indigenous language media that would form the pluralistic and diverse media landscape envisioned in the Windhoek Declaration'. The Charter, however, called on states to promote 'an economic environment that facilitates the development of independent production and diversity in broadcasting'.

The African Charter of Broadcasting contained a specific section on community broadcasting as well as an important section on telecommunications and convergence. The Charter defined community broadcasting as 'for, by and about the community whose ownership is representative of the community, which pursues a social development agenda and which is non-profit.[17] These are by now familiar characteristics. The Charter noted too that the right to communicate included access to telephones, the Internet 'including through the promotion of community-controlled information and communication technology centres'.

Other African policy initiatives included the 2002 media forum of the Bamako conference which addressed the role of the media in the development of the information society, and the 2002 Accra Declaration of the Conference on Africa and the Development Challenges of the twenty-first century. This declaration expressed concern about the widely varying pace of democratisation in different parts of Africa, particularly concerning opportunities for citizen participation and expression.

A range of non-legislative policy actions have been implemented in South Africa in the post-1994 era which collectively have an important impact on the community media sector. They include:
- The Department of Post and Telecommunications has:
  - Licenced more than 80 community radio stations and set aside a frequency spectrum for close to 300 stations.
  - Set up an independent, non-governmental media trust with money from government and donors to support community radio. The IMDT proved unviable and closed down.
  - Licenced a new free-to-air television station and 14 new commercial radio stations.
- The Cultural Industries Growth Strategy was adopted by the Department of Arts, Culture, Science and Technology (DACST) in 1998, prior to its being split into two departments. The policy includes initiatives to stimulate growth in the television and film industry. The strategy investigation showed that income generation depends on the integration of production into a full value chain (Hagg 2002: 33).
- In a Broadcasting Policy Technical Task Team discussion document published in 1998, it was stated: 'A well-founded broadcasting system should ensure pluralities of

---

17 See African Charter on Broadcasting http://www.misgnet.org/broadcast.html

SMALL MEDIA AND THE POLICY ENVIRONMENT

news, views and information. It should give wide and enlightened choices to the citizens and thereby contribute significantly to an effective and vibrant democracy.'[18]
- Municipal Infrastructure Investment Unit (MIIU): The Unit was set up in 1998 to encourage private-sector investment in municipal services and to establish a market for such investments. Government provides an annual grant to the Unit. Through this grant, the Unit has undertaken 15 pilot projects and has assisted many municipalities in preparing and finalising appropriate municipal service partnership agreements. The total number of municipal service partnership transactions completed by the MIIU continues to increase. During 2001/02, the MIIU completed five such projects, with a total contract value of over R1 billion. That brought the total contract value of all MIIU projects during its four-year existence to over R6.7 billion. As a result of just 2001's projects, over 280 000 disadvantaged South African households received new, enhanced, or more efficient municipal services. These services include water and sanitation, waste management, municipal transport and municipal power. The MIIU has embarked on a programme to undertake diagnostic studies in a number of municipalities to determine the opportunity for private-sector investment in these localities.
- Urban Renewal Strategy: The URP falls under the Department of Provincial and Local Government. The programme emphasises three principles:
  - The mobilisation of people so that they can become active participants in their own development;
  - The activities, initiatives and budgetary resources of the three spheres of government should be co-ordinated and focused; and,
  - Public sector investment needs to leverage private sector resources.

  The majority of projects focus on the development of infrastructure in order to address the legacy of apartheid economic development. These projects are co-funded by urban nodal municipalities, provincial governments and national departments. This new system of integrated governance for sustainable development arises from a new current of thinking that emphasises collective responsibility.
- The National Film and Video Foundation (NFVF) was also established by DACST (now split into two departments) to promote and develop the film and television industry in South Africa.
- The DoC has identified, funded and implemented community radio programme production projects including the Community Radio Infrastructure Project as well as capacity building and skills development through the National Electronic Media Institute of South Africa (Nemisa). The department has also 'promised to ensure community media's inclusion in new delivery platforms, ensure community media access to new communications and information technology (Joe Mjwara in CEM Indaba 2001).[19] It also established two bodies in 2001 to advise the minister on digital broadcasting and the development of South African content for the electronic media:
  - The South African Digital Broadcasting Advisory Body (SADBAB), which focuses on opportunities to harness digital technologies and related applications in order to achieve developmental goals, economic growth and job creation, and
  - The South African Broadcast Production Advisory Body (SABPAB), which focuses on strategies for developing and broadcasting more quality local content, especially in the 11 official languages;

---

18 http://www.icasa.org.za
19 Community Electronic Multimedia Indaba, Johannesburg, November 2001

The people's voice

Both the DAC and the Department of Communications have committed to identifying and promoting supply-side initiatives to support production of South African content.

The Universal Service Agency (USA) has established Provincial Telecentre Forums (PTFs) to facilitate interaction.

- Icasa has agreed it 'would support well-organised efforts to establish community multimedia centres and the awarding of multimedia licences in underserviced areas of less than five telephones per 100 households'. These licences, however, are in fact telephone licences to help fill gaps in Telkom's coverage. A number of different definitions of multimedia and the licences that serve it currently exist in South African legislation.
- A spin-off of the RDP's Democratic Information Programme (DIP) was the hosting of a conference in 1996 entitled Empowering Communities in the Information Society, that accepted the notion that multipurpose community development centres were the key instruments in community empowerment. This was developed further in the landmark Information Society and Development (ISAD) conference after which the roll-out of services in poor areas, the launching of MPCCs, citizen post offices, and Public Information Terminals (PiTs) began in earnest.
- The various new initiatives were informed by the government's Integrated Development Strategy (IDS) and also by the Integrated Sustainable Rural Development Strategy (ISRDS) both of which were aimed at ensuring that development was co-ordinated and resources used efficiently. In addition, President Thabo Mbeki used the occasion of his State of the Nation address in 2001 to identify various nodal points at which government departments would be expected to implement their services. According to the national Minister of Communications, Ivy Matsepe-Casaburri: 'As players in the communications sector, we need to follow suit and deploy our resources in a manner that advances the course of integrated development' (CEM Indaba 2001: 10).
- The ISRDS highlights the need for development to reach the large proportion of the South African population who live in the rural areas. The overriding principle of the ISRDS is 'to attain social cohesive and stable communities with viable institutions, sustainable economies and universal access to social amenities able to attract and retain skilled and knowledgeable people equipped to contribute to growth and development'.[20] The policy stresses the participatory and decentralised fashion of successful rural development (as demonstrated by international experience), the need for the integration of development efforts and emphasises the importance of sustainability and the need for the bolstering of local capacity for bottom-up development. These are all key lessons and, indeed, obligations for community media planning and policy. The ISRDS identifies 13 rural nodal points for development.
- *Batho Pele* means people-centred governance. This official slogan underpins much current government policy especially with regard to service delivery.
- ICT and Empowerment Charter: The Information and Communication Technology and Electronics (ICT-E) sector announced in June that it would be drawing up a Black Economic Empowerment (BEE) charter by early 2004. The empowerment charter working group consists of representatives from the Black Information Technology Forum (BITF), Information Industry South Africa (IISA), The South

---

20 See Executive Summary of ISRDS at http://www.lgh/docs/isrds.pdf

Small media and the policy environment

African Communications Forum (SACF), the Information Technology Association (ITA), the Computer Society of South Africa (CSSA), Electronic Industries Federation (EIF) and the South African Chamber of Business (SACOB).

- The DTI is working with the ICT-E sector through the BEE working group and the ICT Development Council, led by Alec Erwin, the Minister of Trade and Industry. Minister Erwin is expected to issue a gazetted code of good practice for the ICT-E sector once the industry reaches an agreement on the ICT and Empowerment charter. The department has compiled a database of BEE companies in the ICT-E sector. The department defines a BEE company as one that is at least 25,1 per cent owned and managed by black people, whether a black firm has control or not.
- A position paper on regional television has been released by Icasa. No further commercial TV licences will be issued for the moment. A position paper on community TV is immanent.
- Almost all major government policy on the media and on ICTs, including the White Paper on Science and Technology (1996), the recommendations of Comtask, the RDP Base Document, the recommendations of the ISAD conference and the Technology Enhanced Learning Investigation (TELI) 1996 call for greater integration of policy initiatives with regard to ICTs and information policy.

A Convergence Bill has now been tabled in Parliament following a national policy colloquium in Johannesburg in July 2003.

2.5 Small media: the law, ethics and the regulators

An extraordinarily high number of the 120 media laws passed during the apartheid era remain on the statute books. This has raised concerns among the media and among non-governmental agencies such as the FXI, and calls persist for these apartheid laws to be scrapped. The FXI has argued that recourse to apartheid legislation has become increasingly common in contemporary South Africa.

Among the apartheid laws still on the statutes is Section 205 of the Criminal Procedures Act that forces journalists to reveal their sources under threat of imprisonment. It is understood that the Centre for Applied Legal Studies (CALS) at the University of the Witwatersrand is compiling an inventory of apartheid laws affecting the media. It is hoped that, in time, these laws will be repealed.

Questions of libel and defamation, however, will continue to be relevant to media organisations in South Africa whether or not the apartheid statutes are removed. Due to its frequent lack of familiarity with media law, the community media sector in particular runs the risk of impinging on them. The severe penalties that can be applied in the wake of libel or defamation infractions pose a very real threat to the survival of community media organisations.

In brief, defamation is a branch of the law (called delict, or tort) that protects a person's reputation. The law of defamation seeks to find a workable balance between the right to an unimpaired reputation and freedom of expression. Any individual is entitled to sue for defamation. In some cases companies or organisations (called 'juristic persons' in law) and even political parties are entitled to sue but the government is expressly forbidden from this course of action.

Since the landmark Bogoshi case in 1998 (National Media Ltd. and others v. Bogoshi 1998 (4) SA 1196(SCA) Supreme Court of Appeal), the application of the law has changed. This was mainly as a result of the advent of the new Constitution which forced the Supreme Court of Appeal to re-examine the issue of defamation cases against the media. The Bogoshi judgment held that a media defendant is not liable for defamation if it was reasonable to publish (or broadcast) the relevant material in that particular way at that particular time. The traditional defences against defamation (that it was the truth, that it was fair comment or that there was qualified privilege) still apply (Maitland 2004).

While the judgment has eased the burden on the media by applying a broad rule of 'reasonableness', defamation can still be a criminal offence (as well as a delict). If the state can prove beyond reasonable doubt that a media organisation has acted unlawfully and with the intention to defame, hefty jail sentences apply.

Aside from court action, however, a number of structures exist which are aimed at ensuring that the media behaves responsibly, fairly and in keeping with the Constitution.

The Press Code of Professional Practice applies to all members of the Forum for Community Journalists (FCJ), the South African National Editors Forum (Sanef), the South African Union of Journalists (SAUJ), the Media Workers Association of South Africa (Mwasa), the Newspaper Association of Southern Africa (NASA) and the Magazine Publishers Association of South Africa (MPASA). The code is premised on the belief that 'vigilant self-regulation is the hallmark of a free and independent press' (POSA 2003). It commits its signatories to report truthfully, accurately and fairly, in a balanced manner and without an intentional or negligent departure from the facts.

The code describes the public interest as the only test that justifies a 'departure from the highest standards of journalism' and includes guidelines on avoiding discrimination, advocacy, comment, the use of confidential sources, payment for articles and the portrayal of violence. The code is enforced by the Press Ombudsman of South Africa (POSA) together with the office's Appeal Panel. Its sanctions include reprimands and the publication of corrections by offending newspapers or magazines.

Historically however, compared to print, broadcasting has always been subject to extensive regulation. The common position is that the right to freedom of expression has traditionally limited government's willingness to regulate print and this component of the sector has consequently been left to its own devices in the open market. Broadcasting, on the other hand, has mostly been part of the public sector and therefore been subject to regulation and protection. The two arguments that convinced most governments to impose restrictive regulations on broadcasting were that there were only a limited number of frequencies available and that broadcasting also was a potentially powerful political tool to be used and developed with care (Van Eijk 1992: 235).

The regulation of community media is a critical question. According to Opubor, regulation is relevant to the promotion of community media precisely because it deals with basic principles and issues concerning ownership, control and the operations of broadcasting and other media (2000: 19). Regulation is far from a simple notion, particularly in the era of globalisation, the Internet, Open Source technology, digitalisation and satellites. There are, however, two different kinds of regulation that impact on community media: control

SMALL MEDIA AND THE POLICY ENVIRONMENT

of the platform or media and access to the market (whether in frequencies, channels or distribution areas), and control of content.

While the equitable allocation of frequencies is a relatively simple task, achieved according to guidelines and agreement, the regulation of content is far more complex. Several codes of conduct, which are currently in operation in the South African media industry, prohibit content that is in effect allowed by the Constitution. An example of this is hate speech, which the Constitution does not ban, but merely fails to protect. Hate speech is prohibited in several codes of conduct. 'The question of what can and can't be said on air is an extremely difficult question indeed to answer,' according to Jane Duncan (1996: 1).

A range of regulatory bodies oversee the functioning of the media in general, and the community media sector in particular. These include:

- *Icasa* is an important regulatory authority with jurisdiction over the small media sector. All broadcast licencees are required to follow the Code of Conduct for Broadcasting Services initially designed by the IBA. The IBA also established an independent Broadcast Monitoring and Complaints Committee (BMCC). The Code of Conduct, which reinforces the freedom to be informed and to receive and pass on opinion, covers such issues as 'sensitive material', truth and accuracy in news presentation, comment and controversy. Election coverage, privacy, paying for information and reporting crime also form part of the code. Icasa also has its own monitoring agency called the Monitoring and Complaints Unit (MCU).

- *The IBA*: in 1998, the IBA issued a discussion paper on revising the Code of Conduct to ensure it was in line with the right of freedom of expression as contained in the 1996 Constitution. The new code has now been legislated in an amendment to the IBA Act. The legislation gives Icasa the responsibility of developing the code. The main principle of the code is the protection of children and it provides specifically for warnings and a watershed period. The IBA has also issued regulations on advertising, infomercials and programme sponsorship (1999), which affirm the underlying principle that the audience must be told when content is sponsored or paid for. The regulations were applicable from 1 April 1999 (advertisements), 1 October 1999 (commercial features) and 1 April 2000 (infomercials and programme sponsorships). It is worth noting that regulations on advertising and sponsorship also raise questions about the sponsorship of certain programmes, in particular news programmes. The regulations, which are currently being challenged by e.tv, prohibit advertising on television news. The position paper noted the need to reassess advertising on radio news after five years. Questions around responsible advertising and sponsorship of children's programming have also been raised. Regulations regarding political party election broadcasts were also framed by the IBA in 1999 and will once again be applicable, though possibly amended, in 2004. The IBA Act (1993) also set out limitations on cross-media ownership. These restrictions included that no person who controlled a newspaper could acquire or retain financial control of both a radio station and hold a television licence. The Act stipulated that where a newspaper represented more than 15 per cent of the total circulation of a particular area, it could not also control a radio station or television licence (if there was substantial overlap of 50 per cent). These limitations are currently being reviewed.

The people's voice

- *The Broadcasting Complaints Committee of South Africa* (BCCSA) was set up by the NAB for sector self-regulation. The BCCSA has a code of conduct.

- *The SAHRC* has already hosted an investigation into racism in the media. In March 2000 the Association of Black Accountants of South Africa claimed that two newspapers (the *Mail & Guardian* and the *Sunday Times*) were racist in the way they reported on what was happening in South Africa. Any citizen may make a complaint to the SAHRC if they feel the media has impinged on human rights as enshrined in the Constitution. If the SAHRC feels a case has been made, it will investigate.

- *The Advertising Standards Authority of South Africa* (ASA) has a code of advertising practice that all broadcasters are obliged to follow. It includes principles such as that advertisements must be legal, decent, honest and truthful, should be prepared with a sense of responsibility and should follow the principles of fair competition. The ASA also has jurisdiction over infomercials. An advertisement, as defined by the IBA, means any content or material broadcast for which the publisher/broadcaster receives a consideration, in cash or otherwise, and which promotes the interest of any person, product or service (IBA Position Paper on Definition of Advertisements, 31 March 1999).

- *The Competition Commission* is charged with ensuring that monopolistic or price collusion practices do not take place in any sector of the economy. The commission, as mentioned above, has not yet investigated the media sector as a memorandum of understanding has been agreed between the Commission and Icasa.

- *The Commission for Gender Equality* (CGE) was established in 1996. Its functions include:
    - Monitoring and evaluating the policies and practices of government, the private sector and other organisations to ensure that they promote and protect gender equality;
    - Public education and information;
    - Reviewing existing and upcoming legislation from a gender perspective;
    - Investigating inequality;
    - Commissioning research and making recommendations to parliament or other authorities;
    - Investigating complaints on any gender related issue; and
    - Monitoring/reporting on compliance with international conventions.

2.6 Universal access and ICT policy

> Information Technology, and the ability to use it and adapt it, is the critical factor in generating and accessing wealth, power and knowledge in our time.
> *Manuel Castells*

The information society of the twenty-first century has seen the emergence of multimedia services, the rapid development of mobile communications, the advent of intelligent networks and satellite communications, according to former minister responsible for Posts

SMALL MEDIA AND THE POLICY ENVIRONMENT

and Telecommunications, Jay Naidoo (1998).[21] Underpinning this increasingly dynamic sector is the common assumption that telecommunications is now a vital driver of economic growth and socio-economic upliftment.

It was the RDP Base Document of 1994 that identified the telecommunications sector as 'an indispensable backbone for the development of all other socio-economic sectors. An effective telecommunications infrastructure, which includes universal access, is essential to enable the delivery of basic services and the reconstruction and development of deprived areas'.[22] By the mid-1990s, the building of an information infrastructure as a prerequisite for national development was gaining international attention (Benjamin 2001: 1). This led to a policy that promoted universal access, a notion central to the Telecommunications Act of 1996. The controversial Act (which went through 14 drafts) also put in place the regulatory framework and policy objectives that determined the future course of the sector in South Africa. Its main objectives included the creation of a universal service fund, the promotion of universal and affordable telecommunications services, the promotion of telecommunications services that are responsive to the needs of users and consumers, and the promotion of fair competition. The Act established both the Universal Service Agency (USA) and the SATRA. The Act was the first major attempt in South Africa to respond to the challenge of using ICTs to promote widespread development (Benjamin 2001: 96).

The question of whether the application of technologies to improve information and communication access can increase the capabilities of disadvantaged and poor people is central to whether the information age will support or undermine development (Benjamin 2001: 1).

The idea of the MPCC first emerged in the early 1980s in Scandinavia (Benjamin 2001: 75). More than 30 different names, like telecentre, have been coined for the concept. After a 'World Telecommunications Development conference' in Buenos Aires in 1994 formally accepted that these telecentres were the ideal method to promote access to telecommunications in developing countries, the idea took off. This was given further emphasis by the influential ISAD (Information Society and Development) Conference in South Africa in 1996. Between 1998 and 2000, seven major international conferences had pushed telecentres as the best telecommunications solution for the developing world. In Africa, two forms of telecentres developed: small, private, commercially-driven phone and communication centres and larger, externally-funded ICT community centres.

While earlier in the 1990s the focus was on providing basic telecommunications, the telecentres were soon seen as the platforms for providing wider access to information systems. Even the notion of universal access and universal service began to change. According to Dipuo Mvelase, USA CEO, the historical concepts of universal service and universal access 'have been broadened beyond basic telephony to encompass other services delivered by modern ICT infrastructure' (CEMI 2001: 41).

Benjamin notes, however, that the prominence of the information age and the perceived importance of ICTs made telecentres particularly attractive to government. This sparked an unseemly and damaging battle for turf between the DoC, the DTI and the DACST (Benjamin 2001: 99). There was also overlap between the regulatory bodies SATRA and the

---

21 Speech on 'Investment in the SA Telecommunications Sector' given on 7 December 1998. See http://www.gcis.gov.za
22 Cited in 'An Information Policy Handbook for Southern Africa'. See http://www.dbsa.org/publications/ictpolsa.index.html

The people's voice

Universal Service Agency (USA) as well as some confusion over the mandate for the USF. 'By May 2000, the USA was dispirited and disillusioned ... SATRA also had many problems' (Benjamin 2001: 104). The merger of SATRA and the IBA caused further complications particularly when combined with a cut in funding.

In late March 2001, the Cabinet approved a number of policy directives with regard to telecommunications policy. This followed a national colloquium of shareholders on the subject. Key elements of the directives acknowledged that the touchstones of policy with regard to ICTs are the following: BEE, domestic and foreign direct investment, stable and predictable regulation, universal access and service, HRD and a reduced digital divide.

2.7 Small media: labour and skills development

The passage of a whole raft of laws concerning skills and training are inevitably going to impact on the small media sector. This is true not only in the way in which small media units are organised but also in the way in which training is accessed and provided. The South African Qualifications Act (1995), the Skills Development Act (1998) and employment equity legislation will, according to Dave Thomas, former CEO of the Media, Advertising, Publishing, Printing and Packaging Sector Education and Training Authority (MAPPP SETA) 'completely recast the educational and training landscape in the country' (Steenveld 2002: 76).

In Thomas's view, the levy imposed on employers (together with the possibility of reclaiming a portion of the levy) will have the effect of elevating the status of training in companies. The importance of ongoing training is furthermore emphasised by employment equity laws with companies obliged to file their plans and targets with government (Steenveld 2002: 77).

The NQF is intended to eliminate division between vocational and academic education, recognise 'real world' learning and ensure that training institutions are accountable by providing an outcomes-based orientation. Once the system has been established, flexible and appropriate qualifications will be in place that can be awarded by a range of entities. It is anticipated that learnerships will serve as a work-based route to qualifications.

It is evident that a great deal of uncertainty and ignorance pervades the media industry concerning the devising and implementation of qualifications and learnerships (Hadland & Voorbach 2003: 19). Very few of even the mainstream media's managers appeared to be aware of the SAQA process in anything but the most vague or general terms. This is almost certain to be the case in the smaller media sector. With the first unit standards already approved and the first national diploma qualification (sub-editing) in place, the Standards Generating Bodies (SGBs) at work in the sector are beginning to make progress.

A couple of different implications of the NQF are becoming discernible. First, a dramatic increase in paperwork is already being experienced by training providers. This is putting pressure on administrative capacity. Second, while the NQF is intended to weed out the fly-by-night training organisations that have multiplied quickly in recent years, there is likely to be a rush to provide accredited courses once national diplomas and unit standards are implemented. Consolidation in the sector, in the views of some analysts, is inevitable (Hadland & Voorbach 2002: 20).

Small media and the policy environment

Government policy places great importance on HRD as an integral part of the overall developmental needs of the country. The South African NQF was developed as part of a strategy for the implementation of human resource development.

The data gathering that was part of this project indicates the involvement of no less than three SETAs in the local media sector: the Information Systems, Electronic and Telecommunications Technologies Sector Education and Training Authority (ISETT SETA), the Manufacturing, Engineering and Related Services Sector Education and Training Authority (MERS SETA) and MAPPP SETA.

2.8 Small media and the global experience

The community media sector has been thriving in many parts of the world for nearly 50 years and a large body of experience and many lessons have been learned in this period. To give an idea of the scope of community media, there are an estimated 2 billion radio receivers and 20 000 radio stations worldwide (Fraser 2002: 69). But it is equally true that the development of community media has been deeply uneven across the globe. In some parts, access to community media is simple and frequent. Latin America has the largest number of community radio stations with well over 4 000 (Siemering 1997: 2). In other parts, such as India, there is no community media at all. In the Indian case, the government is apparently worried about secessionist groups and subversive propaganda (Ninan, 2000: 31).

Depending on the part of the world we are examining, the functions and origins of the community sector are different. In the United States, for instance, community radio was established as an alternative to entertainment-oriented programming and 'middle-of-the-road' conformist stations. In Europe, it was the opposite. Community radio got going in Europe due to the lack of entertainment programming and the prevalence of light music radio (Hollander in Jankowski et al. 1992: 7).

What has been common is an anti-establishment attitude by which the state or prevailing opinion is challenged by the diversity of voices that community media is so capable of presenting. This is true in Bolivia – where the tin miners established the first radio station in the 1940s – in France, the United States and in many other places. In extremely few cases does the community media act principally as an agent of government information and still retain its capacity to represent the interests and voices of its constituency.

Community media organisations everywhere have consistently been confronted by zealous regulators and by monopolistic state tendencies, particularly concerning broadcasting. Radio transmission experiments that began in the wake of World War I led to many countries in western Europe investigating the establishment of broadcasting systems. National governments felt regulation was necessary to avoid uncontrolled growth in the number of radio stations as well as the allocation of frequencies from the limited spectrum (Hollander in Jankowski et al. 1992: 7). All the national broadcasting systems that developed at this time were monopolistic and held the exclusive right to nationwide radio and television programming. By the 1950s, post-war economic growth, the availability and cheap cost of transistor radios, improved technology (more powerful transmitters and the emergence of FM radio) led to a rise in audiences and an improvement in the quality of programming. It also spawned the rise of alternative, independent media sometimes funded by listeners. These outlets were frequently more willing to air controversial programming.

Television was introduced to western Europe in the 1950s but the real explosion occurred in the 1960s when the number of television sets increased exponentially. The move from black and white television to colour combined with the economic recession of the 1970s led to stagnation in the television sector at this time which corresponded with the rise of various social reform movements pushing for greater levels of participation. Community radio and television emerged in the mid-1970s by which time satellite television, pay television and pirate radio and television had sparked major debate within the sector.

The community print media has proved resilient, cost-effective and has become an essential component of community cohesion, identity and communications in many countries.

During the course of this paper we have made many references to international research on the community media sector. Let us examine here some of the specific lessons that have been forthcoming from the global community sector, drawn from the latest international research:

- Community media succeeds best where it is simply an added tool to enhance already high levels of community development awareness (Cholmondeley 2000: 111). The same conclusions have been made with community television: 'There can only be real community television in a locality where community relations are already alive and active' (Lundby in Jankowski et al. 1992: 30). The underlying lesson here is that the community media cannot and should not be used to establish community cohesion or be imposed on areas of low community awareness or activism. It should, instead, be built on the social capital, structures and organisation that already exist.
- There is no substitute for the highest levels of community participation. This is true from the conception and the drawing up of business plans to day-to-day operations. 'Every effort to involve the target communities at every stage of development ... has paid dividends in terms of the levels of trust, support and participation by the community' (Cholmondeley 2000: 111).
- 'Community radio and community television provide an alternative to the mainstream media, but their institutional forms influence the programming they can offer. Their small size limits their ability to produce their own in-house programming and their independence and fragmentation inhibits the sharing of what programming they do produce. Community radio's solution has been to turn to externally-produced programming. However, when it imports news and public affairs it often becomes a repeater for the biases of producers who are owned or funded by large business interests. Community television, with much fewer options for programme importation, often leaves channels underutilised' (Klein 1999: 50).
  Klein suggests three solutions:
  - The creation of a dedicated organisation to generate programming for the community media sector.
  - The pooling and national distribution of existing local programming.
  - The creation and utilisation of non-profit distributors (such as DeepDish TV, a satellite service, and Free Speech TV, which provides video-tapes) (1999: 50).
- The ideal audience for a community radio station is between five and twenty thousand. Any less, is unsustainable, any more, too diffuse (Fraser & Restrepo-Estrada 2002: 72).

- A precise methodology for evaluating the impact of community radio based on appropriate social indicators has still to be devised (Fraser & Restrepo-Estrada 2002: 72).
- Klein notes that within community media organisations, a lack of awareness of outside programming sources, responsibilities of the staff and a variety of small, administrative barriers are often sufficient to prevent the organisation accessing material that is already available. He argues that the presence of community media activists is an essential component of an enabling environment (Klein 1999: 50).
- In recent years there has been a gradual liberalisation of media and a growing phenomenon of community media in Africa. However, many of the existing and emerging community media do not possess the economic, technological or human resources required for sustainability (Boafo 2000: 5). In fact, the Unesco writers demonstrate that community media are not likely to be sustainable from the point of view of the hosting/owning community, though new technologies (such as multimedia centres) may make this possible by cutting costs (Boafo 2000: 5).
- There is a growing, urgent importance to collaborate and co-ordinate policy with regional authorities and organisations. This gains even more credence against the background of digitisation and satellite telecommunication technologies and as the audiences of local media organisations begin to overlap particularly on or near international borders.
- The New Plan for African Development (Nepad) has major implications for the South African media sector and in particular for public broadcasting, according to the FXI: 'Its provisions about restoring and maintaining macroeconomic stability and increasing private sector investment in infrastructure could undo any attempts to establish publicly-owned and controlled and public-funded public broadcasting' (FXI Annual Report 2001/2002: 11).[23] Nepad also has important consequences for the realisation of universal service and universal access in relation to ICTs ... including a telecommunications system that is increasingly unable to offer affordable services, hence the massive rate of churn (FXI Annual Report 2001/2002: 11).[24]
- Liberalised trade and the increased global flow of capital are major driving factors for any country. This gains particular significance in the status of cultural goods and services assigned by the General Agreement on Tariffs and Trade (GATT) and by the World Trade Organisation (WTO). The United States calls for a totally free and open market in cultural products. Unesco (Stockholm Action Plan of 1998), on the other hand, argues that 'cultural goods and services should be fully recognised and treated as not being like other forms of merchandise' (Discussion paper on Review of Local Content Quotas, Icasa, Dec 2000: 31).[25] The international Network on Cultural Policy (representing 50 countries, including South Africa) has adopted Unesco's view and, in addition, recognises the right of governments to establish their cultural policies freely. Should the US lobby succeed in amending WTO policy, this could have serious implications on, for instance, local content quotas (Discussion Paper on Review of Local Content Quotas, Icasa Dec 2000: 31). GATT also impacts on intellectual property rights.
- The prospect of creating national networks of local radio stations has revived a commercial interest in community radio in some parts of the world. The danger of such networks, however, is the commercial usurpation that accompanies such close ties and even dependency on advertising and commercial interests.

---

23 http//www.fxi.org.za
24 http//www.fxi.org.za
25 http://www.icasa.org.za

- The potential of digital technology has opened up a realm of new possibilities for the small media sector.
- Satellite broadcasting has become a key phenomenon in broadcasting globally, compelling regulatory regimes all over the world to renew their policies.
- Four key developments are anticipated in the small media sector in the next phase of the twenty-first century:
  - There will be a rapid growth in regional regulations and standards.
  - The commercialisation of programming (in particular through advertising) is inevitable.
  - Small media organisations can be expected to increase in the scale of their operations. In the broadcast sector, this is likely to be accompanied by a tendency toward increased transmission power.
  - The development of networking has been identified as an increasingly prominent factor in the small media sector (Van Eijk in Jankowski et al. 1992: 243).
- The ubiquitous phenomenon of convergence has signalled an equally widespread move in the small media sector toward multimedia platforms and functions.
- In global terms, convergence has become a very real and important shift in the media sector in general. Should there be any doubt, consider the following: In the last three years Reuters (the world's largest news provider) has spent about R8 billion converting itself into an Internet company. The Tribune Company, one of the largest news organisations in the United States, has created a central newsroom that cuts across media boundaries, gathering news and distributing it to print, broadcast and Internet outlets in one operation. The *Financial Times* of London has recently integrated its print and online services into one newsroom (AEJMC 2000: 19). Closer to home, take note of Moneyweb, a listed company which recently concluded a deal to supply television programming to e.tv and daily content to the *Citizen* newspaper in addition to its existing print (newsletter), radio and Internet products.
- Finally, the impact of cellphone video technology on news coverage is already being felt in some countries, such as Japan, where every person with a cellphone has the potential to become an eyewitness reporter.

Many of these matters came to a head at the first round of the World Summit on the Information Society (WSIS), in Geneva in 2003. The summit was led by the International Telecommunications Union (ITU) and had as its aim 'to develop a common vision and understanding of the Information Society, to better understand its scope and dimensions and to draw up a strategic plan of action for successfully adapting to the new society'.[26] The second phase of WSIS is scheduled for 2005 in Tunis, following which a declaration and action plan will be adopted.

The summit has spawned a range of organisations and networks, including Voices 21 and CRIS (Communication Rights in the Information Society) that are seeking to reaffirm the role of community media in countering the negative impacts of globalisation. Key voices in the campaign include Sean O'Siochru and Cees J Hamelink. The campaign, which proposes a People's Communication Charter and the entrenchment of the fundamental rights to communication and to cultural production, seeks to protect the rights of civil society in government and corporate-led policy platforms such as WSIS and the ITU.

---

26 http://www.itu.int/wsis

SMALL MEDIA AND THE POLICY ENVIRONMENT

Community media, in other words, has become a global movement. It is being held up as an antidote to the overarching commercialism and homogeneity of a globalising world. The opportunities inherent in this development include the presence of networks, NGOs and groupings keen to support and foster the development of community media, particularly in the developing world. It would be a mistake to assume that the community media in South Africa inhabit an isolated realm at the periphery of global policy formulation. In fact, recognition of the role of the community media in bolstering people's fundamental rights is growing all the time.

2.9 Parallel initiatives

There are a host of current, parallel initiatives that are of relevance to the small media sector. One guestimate suggests these projects have been implemented in excess of 5 000 different sites across South Africa.[27] These need to be noted by the MDDA and efforts made to participate in the policy-creation and decision-making surrounding these initiatives:
- The GCIS has established 60 MPCCs with another 60 in the pipeline;
- The Universal Service Agency (USA): The USA has established about 60 telecentres, 22 cyberschools and 20 Web-Internet Laboratories (WILs);
- The DoC has established 115 PiTs/Dotzas together with 41 Arts and Culture centres. It also has a content project headed by Nemisa, and a Digitalisation Project;
- The Pan South African Language Board (Pansalb) has a range of relevant programmes and priorities;
- Commission for the Promotion and Protection of Cultural and Linguistic Minorities: The last Chapter 9 body will soon begin functioning;
- The Department of Science and Technology (DST) has recently offered a tender for an arts and science centre strategy;
- Schools projects: Estimated to number in the region of 3 500 projects involving telecommunications and computing in schools;
- Various projects under the ambit of the departments of Home Affairs, Social Services and Welfare;
- National Intersectoral Steering Committees (NISSCs), provincial (PISSC) and local (LISSC), are currently intervening in the sector under GCIS with special reference to MPCCs;
- GCIS is also investigating video resource centres and a news network;
- In the private sector: Nortel, Mweb, Digital Villages, ISPA, Vodacom (2 200 phone shops) and Liberty Life are among those embarking on private sector initiatives;
- The NCRF is involved in support for community radio and has proposed a hub system for regional collaboration;
- The South African Community Radio Information Network (SACRIN) is a radio programme exchange project;
- InfoLit sites: about 25 of these are in operation;
- SCAT: 15 projects;
- The South African NGO Coalition (Sangoco): 1 200 sites;
- Sentech is issuing multimedia licences;
- Kaizer Chiefs: efforts are afoot to connect the biggest supporters' club in South Africa;
- Two regional protocols have been established for community television, through the DoC and Icasa;

27 CMS Task Team discussion, October 2003

The people's voice

- The DTI: There is much work on SMMEs taking place within DTI, including the issuing of multimedia licences to SMMEs in under-serviced areas;
- Icasa is investigating privately-owned regional television licences. A discussion document is imminent;
- DStv: is pursuing educational television initiatives through channels 82 and 83;
- The State Information Technology Agency (SITA) was established in January 1999 to tackle government's IT problems. SITA is a collaboration between the Department of State Expenditure, Department of Defence and SA Police Service;
- The SETA gateway project;
- South African Industrial Strategy Project (SAITIS): a DTI project, begun in 1999, aimed at evaluating the status of ICTs and their usage;
- ICT Sector Development Framework (November, 2000): a consequence of SAITIS aimed at stimulating growth of the ICT industry in South Africa;
- Soon to come: Microsoft, Gauteng Online, Khanya, and projects by the KwaZulu-Natal Provincial government and Northern Cape schools;
- Java Planet: a DoC initiative to train Java programmers; and
- WILs: Web-Internet Laboratories, a DoC project which has seen the creation of almost 100 Internet laboratories with 20 PCs, a printer, access to the Internet, digital camera, television and VCR in learning institutions.

3 Overview of small media in South Africa

3.1 Introduction

Until this report was compiled, no satisfactory national database of all South African small media organisations existed. Different stakeholders held partial versions that were frequently out-of-date, incomplete or referred to only one of the different branches of community media. From the database, it is now possible to sketch the topography of the sector. The collection of material for the database of community media organisations in South Africa has produced some interesting and, in a few cases, quite unexpected results that are discussed below.

Included in the topography, this chapter also describes the current status of each of the components of the sector, including the service providers, discusses the need to move away from technologically determined solutions, and debates the future of community multimedia services.

Topography of local media
There are an estimated 246 small media organisations in South Africa at present. It is still necessary to estimate as some organisations simply could not be contacted, even though they already possessed, for example, a community radio licence. Others were such small operations, consisting of one or two people with irregular publishing frequency from changing locations, that they could not be tracked down in the several months allotted to data capturing.

In terms of operational status, the 246 organisations can be categorised as:
- Not currently in operation, but hope to resume their work   22
- 'Emerging' in that they have existed for less than 18 months   50
- Fully-functioning, contactable local media operations   174

The fully-functioning organisations can be broken down as follows:
- Print   83
- Radio   81
- Audio-visual/multimedia   10

In terms of legal status, two-thirds of print organisations are commercial for-profit operations and one third are non-profit/Section 21 organisations. In the radio sector, the overwhelming majority are non-profit/Section 21 compared to a small number of Pty. Ltd. or ccs. The multimedia operations were split roughly in half. In a few cases, organisation representatives did not know the current legal status. These organisations were omitted from the calculations.

These figures indicate quite clearly that in spite of a considerable bias in the channelling of funding and support to the community radio sector in recent years, a greater number of community print organisations continue to operate in the country. While these print outlets may not reach as large an audience compared to radio, their persistence makes a powerful argument for their status and importance within communities. Community or independent print organisations continue to serve a valued function within communities and are kept going by high levels of volunteerism.

A total of 28 organisations currently provide services to the small media sector in South Africa. Of these 28 service providers, 19 took part in this research and answered detailed questionnaires on their activities, budgets, services and understanding of the dynamics and challenges of the sector. The 19 service providers that did participate represent all the major players and, collectively, manage an annual budget in excess of R40 million. Several funders were also questioned on their work in the sector.

The service providers for the small media sector can be divided into the following eight categories:
- Networks;
- News/photographic agencies;
- Training centres;
- Policy/research/advocacy;
- Media monitoring;
- Content development;
- Distribution; and
- Technical support.

The sector is strong on accommodating people with disabilities and runs projects largely nationally but also some that reach the region and the continent. Each service provider employs, on average, five full-time staffers with a total employment figure of about 300 (19 service providers reported a total staff of 294: of these 178 were full-time and 116 part-time).

From the data provided, the organisations making up the service provider sector are able to assess the needs of their target groups effectively and are in constant liaison and consultation with them. They generally have strong boards that are frequently a healthy mix of expertise and target group/beneficiary representation. Many of the organisations are working with 'communities of interest' with women and youth being popular target groups.

It is important to note that many service providers also produce media and have a serious claim to be considered part of, as well as providing services to, the small media sector. Armed with the capacity to make a real impact, producing a significant output of media products and already representing at least a third of the budgetary value of the sector, the service providers are a critically important factor in the small media sector.

The community and independent media sector has a total annual expenditure of around R115 million (including the service provider component representing about R40 million) and employs about 1 000 people full-time and roughly 4 000 part-time or as volunteers. Some small media organisations reported they regularly made use of 40 volunteers or more, suggesting the 4 000 estimate is probably conservative.

The case study research, which focused in-depth on 25 different small media organisations, confirms that, in general terms, South Africa's small media sector is functioning in socio-economic circumstances that are extremely difficult. All reported high levels of joblessness, poverty and the symptoms of social breakdown in their areas. All complained of the difficulties of securing adequate resources, training and assistance.

As harsh as conditions generally are in the sector, there are undoubted strengths among those involved in producing media for their communities. These include their high degree of motivation, their self-reliance, their connectedness with their communities, their passion for producing media, and their preference for collective decision-making.

Overview of small media in South Africa

Participating in community media organisations, as frustrating as it can sometimes be, is also an undeniably empowering experience on all sorts of levels. Poor gender representivity was noted not only among the staff of the case studies profiled in the sector, but also among their boards.

For all forms of small media, a combination of hard work, community support and cost-effective service provision were cited as being the three main reasons for success. According to one respondent: 'We provide a service that even the poorest of the poor can afford or even get free. We try to educate the people and keep them informed with what is happening around them.'

A more detailed analysis can be found in the next chapter. To complete the topographical overview, here are a few remarks on the current state of the constituent parts of the sector.

3.2 Community radio

Community media has become synonymous in many people's minds with community radio. This is because radio is seen as an ideal medium as it is affordable, easy to install and operate, and people don't need to be able to read or write to access information. From the first pronouncement on progressive media policy back at the Jabulani! Freedom of the Airwaves Conference in 1991, community broadcasting was considered one of the three tiers of the South African broadcasting system along with public broadcasting and private broadcasting. This structure was formalised in the 1993 IBA Act where the notion of community broadcasting was further subdivided into radio and television services.

The Cassette Education Trust, which later merged with Bush Radio, became the training ground for the incipient community radio movement. The NCRF was formed in 1993 in Orlando, Soweto, in order to 'lobby for the diversification of the airwaves in South Africa, and to foster a dynamic broadcasting environment in the country through the establishment of radio stations' (NCRF brochure). Arguably, what followed was one of the greatest achievements in the democratisation of media in South Africa in the past decade: the licensing of about 100 community radio stations. Of these, most are broadcasting successfully, offering a variety of programmes and serving a valuable community service. The majority are operated by and for historically disadvantaged communities. In 1991, it was estimated that there were over 1.6 million listeners, spread across every province of the country (Dooms, 2002: 1).

Some of the more significant and positive developments in the community radio sector include:
- The NCRF's Sacrin facilitates programme exchange via satellite, linking more than 30 community radio stations which get paid for local programmes they produce, or national satellite feeds they carry, on public education topics.
- Many community radio stations are beginning to position themselves as an interface between poor communities and the Internet. This is illustrated by the increased usage by radio stations of ICTs as a tool to enhance information-gathering, programme production, programme sharing and information exchange within the sector.
- The NCRF's Hub Plan aims to promote improved networking, collaboration and support between community radio stations at a provincial level to facilitate, among other things, skills transfer and procurement.

THE PEOPLE'S VOICE

- A significant contribution by the community radio NQF, under the auspices of the MAPPP SETA.
- Various content development initiatives which are aimed at delivering programme production skills at a local level around important social justice issues, in partnership with larger national NGOs such as Idasa, Agenda and Workers World Radio. The sector has been very successful at securing programme sponsorship which points to future donor trends.
- A partnership with the GCIS through which radio stations are paid to flight government information, sent via the Sacrin satellite feed.
- The DoC-led initiative to provide broadcasting equipment to community radio stations as well as funding for programming tackling gender, HIV/AIDS and disability issues. Many of the interviewees from this study argued this role should, in future, be transferred to the MDDA.
- The sectors ability to maintain a high profile and advance the interests of its members in the numerous, ongoing policy and legislative process.

Despite these positive developments in community radio, many challenges remain. Institutional weaknesses continue to beset the sector, particularly in the areas of management and administration. Often an inability to pay staff adequately leads to a blurring of roles between the board, staff and volunteers. Licencing delays, caused by the IBA/SATRA merger, has caused further disruption, including high board turnover and community disillusionment (Dooms 2002: 2).

Financially, community radio stations face considerable challenges. These include a lack of skills in planning, budgeting and fund-raising report writing skills. While some stations are having a degree of success at tapping into local business for advertising and sponsorship, this is the exception rather than the rule. A shortfall of skills in advertising and marketing is compounded by a lack of support from local (predominantly white) business. The limited broadcast radius imposed on many stations by their licence conditions does little to alleviate this. Many stations operate in such poor, remote communities that they can never hope to become self-sustainable.

Many stations are struggling with inappropriate or incorrectly installed studio and transmission equipment. Staff have received little training in operations and maintenance and many stations are located in areas where there is no support if equipment breaks down.

More and more, community radio stations are in the firing line for failing to fulfil their role as a tool for change and development. The term 'community radio' is often used loosely to describe media that targets black, working class communities. No doubt this reflects the current, and indeed pressing, priority to redress apartheid imbalances in the media and promote media diversity. But community media, by true, historical definition is much more than that. It is a platform to encourage and promote dialogue, social change and development.

Community radio stations frequently mimic their privately owned counterparts. Beyond annual meetings and talk shows, many have failed to develop the necessary ties with local NGOs, community based organisations (CBOs) and civic structures. These ties would have brought them closer to the communities they serve and enabled them to produce

OVERVIEW OF SMALL MEDIA IN SOUTH AFRICA

programming of a more participatory and developmental nature. The emphasis on quality programming does not take into account the importance of process, whereby ordinary people are able to access the station and exercise their right to communicate. While committed to creating programming for development and empowerment purposes, they often lack the skills and resources to make any real impact in this area. The absence of partnerships with local government, integrated development planning and other community structures has placed limitations on the extent to which community radio has been able to facilitate community participation in local government and development initiatives.

3.3 Print media

One of the most interesting results of the research carried out in this project has been that there are roughly the same number of small print projects in South Africa (around 80) as radio projects, despite the very skewed channelling of funds and resources in favour of the latter. The once vibrant oppositional print media is a shadow of its former self and is struggling to survive. Since the demise of virtually all of the small media organisations associated with the struggle era, including veteran publications such as *Learn and Teach*, *Grassroots* and *Saamstaan*, along with their networks Community Media Network (Comnet) and, later, Community Print Sector of South Africa (Copssa) in the late 1990s, there have been three notable developments regarding the development of local print media. These include:

- The combination of emerging black print media enterprises and not-for profit print organisations, otherwise known as 'new publishers' supported by the PDU.
- The emergence of a range of community newsletters, often working in partnership with government departments, aimed at promoting a two-way flow of communications between government and communities.
- The IMA, formed in 2003, which represents 78 community and independent print media formations. Working with a string of 42 freelancers, the organisation acts primarily as a news agency.

3.3.1 The Print Development Unit

The PDU was established as an 'interim development unit' (prior to the establishment of the MDDA) in February 2000 with a focus on developing support strategies to assist in the growth of the emerging print media sector. The unit was funded by the five major, mainstream print media houses that make up PMSA and which dominate the South African print media sector as a whole.

The PDU adopted a dual strategy consisting of:
- A training programme designed to meet the training needs of publishers; and
- A survey of the sector aimed at developing a 'model of viable publishing'. The results of this survey were produced in a report entitled *New Markets, New Readers, New Publishers*.

During the course of its three years of existence the PDU had contact with 57 publications, although at least 26 of these ceased to exist or could no longer be traced during the period. The PDU developed a methodology for extending training and support to new publishers that reflects the approach of many other training service providers operating in the sector. It identified four broad areas of development: financial and management systems, advertising and marketing, editorial and design, and information technology. The latter was never implemented due to limited resources. Operating with two full-time staff and four consultants, each specialising in the above areas, support took the form of a number of on-site visits, including needs assessments, staff training, setting targets, monitoring and mentoring. In addition, staff were encouraged to attend the central training programme, consisting of short courses, offered by the PDU in Johannesburg.

The *New Publishers* report states that 'the PDU and its intellectual heritage clearly represent the values of market driven development'. Viewed from within the limits of this perspective, the report puts forward some useful recommendations on how new publishers could be supported including:
- A press card accreditation system for new publisher staff;
- An interactive website promoting access to key stakeholders such as advertisers, marketers and other print media companies;
- An online news agency;
- Improved systems for circulation verification;
- Collective printing procurement;
- A management service to assist with a range of business issues; and
- A national advertising procurement agency.

As its central tenet, the report speaks of the importance of 'reinventing the (emerging press) into an entrepreneurial one – community-centred newsgathering (being) the key to successful press entrepreneurship in the current era – attracting both readers and the advertisers who seek to reach them' (PDU, 2002: 7). While the authors of this report believe that community media need to be more business-minded and commercial media more community orientated, we do not advocate that community media should transform itself into a 'market driven' model, as the PDU suggests. We feel this would contradict the values that underpin community media worldwide as discussed extensively in Chapter 2.

The PDU cites the emergence of a black middle class and rapid urbanisation as major opportunities for the growth of new publishers. While this is no doubt true, this 'cherry picking' approach offers no solutions for media serving poor, marginalised or rural communities. Clearly, the profit oriented, market driven model has its limitations when it comes to promoting a truly equitable and diverse media landscape. Although it certainly has its place on the list of possible solutions, it is by no means the one and only 'cure-all'.

The PDU makes some suggestions on the need to build 'ethical and mutually advantageous' partnerships between new publishers and the mainstream media (2002: 9). This is in direct response to repeated complaints by the community radio sector and new publishers that staff, once trained and experienced, are recruited by larger press competitors offering higher salaries and perks. The PDU further suggests the development of a voluntary Code of Practice to regulate the relationships between the new publishers and the industry. The authors broadly support these suggestions and allude to them in our own concluding chapter.

OVERVIEW OF SMALL MEDIA IN SOUTH AFRICA

3.3.2 Small print media and government

We have already mentioned in this report efforts to establish community newspapers or 'municipal newsletters', often within MPCCs, as a significant development as far as small print media is concerned. These initiatives generally involve a two-way partnership between community structures and various government departments (including local government, provincial government and the GCIS) and are primarily seen as a means of facilitating the two-way flow of information and communication between government and citizens.

While these initiatives have been quite successful at unlocking government resources, the challenge will be to ensure these newsletters do not simply perpetuate the 'top-down' flow of information from government to community. It is also important they are able to facilitate dialogue within the community itself and enable civic structures to communicate back to government, i.e. a horizontal and vertical, two-way flow of information.

This model also raises interesting questions about the ownership and control of these newsletters. Are they an official government communications vehicle, a government/community partnership or are they owned and controlled by the community, as in the case of community radio? And what are the implications for editorial control and independence? The issue of government's relationship to community media is considered in more detail in Chapter 4.

In terms of sustainability, community or municipal newsletters have a better chance of survival due to the support of government, which naturally brings with it financial and other resources. The challenge will be to tap into other local resources such as adspend from local business.

3.3.3 The Independent Media Association

The IMA is a collection of more than 70 print based, small commercial outfits – many of which are based in the rural areas – that was established in early 2003. The alliance is a lobby group that takes up projects in the interest of its members, including
- Syndication of articles generated by the association's members;
- Joint ventures;
- Information on funding sources;
- Negotiating for free legal assistance from large media law firms;
- Negotiating compensation when head-hunting deprives small operators of key staff;
- Better access to government advertising;
- Discounted software; and
- Facilitating access to relevant, practical training.

A current concern of the IMA is the lack of an independent advertising clearing house for independent print media. (The IMA is at <http://www.media-alliance.org.za>)

3.4 Community audiovisual media

Community audiovisual media has its roots in the anti-apartheid liberation movement. Since the new, democratic government came into power in 1994, many of the proponents of community audiovisual media have been absorbed into government or the private sector.

THE PEOPLE'S VOICE

Despite a difficult policy and funding environment, some established organisations still remain active in this area. Whether or not these can be defined as 'community media' in the strict definition of the term is open to debate. Many of the organisations are also responding to the dire need for HRD for the audiovisual industry as a whole. Some of the current players in the sector include:

- The 25-year-old CVET focuses on training, access to production facilities and exhibition/visual literacy.
- New initiatives such as the Apollo Development Association in Victoria West point to the viability and need for audiovisual training and production opportunities in rural communities.
- Molweni is a township-based production collective incorporating tourism and a festival. It grew out of CVET.
- The Film Resource Unit (FRU) distributes and exhibits development-oriented content.
- The Newtown Film and Television School is training a new generation of black independent filmmakers.

The notion of community television (CTV) was enshrined in the IBA Act of 1993, creating enormous expectations among media activists and community structures that an enabling environment for community access to this powerful medium would be created. At the Community Media 2000 conference in Cape Town, the Open Window Network (OWN) was formed to take forward the building of a community and development oriented audio-visual media sector in South Africa.

The costs involved in setting up CTV presented a huge challenge. OWN conducted research into the structure and viability of CTV resulting in the proposal of various hybrid models. One model envisaged decentralised access to video, on a digital platform, built on the back of the country's 'national information infrastructure' (within MPCCs and telecentres) and linked to a national digital signal distribution network. Another model was developed in partnership with Orbicom whereby programming would be shared via satellite among a network of community television consortia. A third model devised by Mike Aldridge envisaged what was called a 'C-PEG model' by which CTV is established as a partnership between government and educational institutions, including a 'public access' and commercial programming segment (Aldridge 2003).

Recognising that it may take some time for these ambitious models to become a reality, CTV activists lobbied the SABC to provide 'public access time slots' on the former regional services. After years of lobbying, the SABC eventually agreed and signed a 'Declaration of Intent' in May 1996. This opened up huge economic opportunities for CTV as it was now in a position to generate an income from advertising and sponsorship for programme production. As a result, CTV found its role, in the short term, as a strategy to promote diverse access to video training and production opportunities. A series of successful test transmissions was undertaken in Durban and Cape Town.

The serious need for human resource development in the audio-visual sector generated many challenging debates on the use of different models for CTV in the South African context. While many feel strongly that CTV is not the domain of the independent production sector, others argue that community audio-visual media should be viewed as a training ground for new entrants into the film and television industry.

Out of these debates emerged the call for a 'Workshop Movement', similar to that in the United Kingdom in the 1970s. The idea was to have one 'video access centre' per province. The centres were intended to serve as development nodes for community audio-visual media as well as provide space for the training and development of emerging independent filmmakers. The CVET and the KwaZulu-Natal Community Video Access Centre (KZN C-VAC) are seen as the forerunners of this movement.

After initially sending positive signals, Icasa has continually postponed its legislative mandate to undertake the research into CTV. The initial impetus for CTV has since waned significantly due to a lack of support among policymakers and because of the loss of many of its key proponents to the private sector. The flagship KZN C-VAC has closed down. The activities of OWN have been seriously curtailed through a lack of funding. The organisation is currently not contactable. The CTV sector of old is dormant, waiting for an opportunity to resuscitate.

Many believe that it is not viable to introduce CTV as a 'stand alone' concept, but that CTV should be integrated into other strategies to extend universal access to ICTs and the media in general. As the database from this study illustrates, this is already starting to happen with the emergence of multimedia centres, which include, but are not limited to video, such as the Apollo Development Association (video and ICTs) and the CBO network. Video is also increasingly becoming a feature of CACs.

In discussing video, the training and production aspects are often over emphasised, whereas, in fact, improving distribution is an equally important and realistic short-term goal. The FRU is doing some important work setting up Video Resource Centres (VRCs) in rural areas. More recently, the FRU, in partnership with the GCIS, plans to set up VRCs in MPCCs, including facilities for video production.

Organisations such as 'Steps' are developing an alternative, grassroots distribution strategy for films dealing with HIV/AIDS. Other organisations, such as CVET and Mediaworks, are setting up 'film/media clubs' in schools with the dual goal of promoting visual literacy and audience development. The clubs offer a basic introduction to video production and school screenings. Interestingly, almost half of the organisations that participated in the case studies of this project had television sets and video machines, making them ideal sites for the introduction of VRCs. Discussions have also taken place on the notion of a 'net-casting' pilot project to be conducted by Mike Aldridge in collaboration with the GCIS and a group of MPCCs and other NGOs in the Western Cape.

3.5   The future: community multimedia services?

The low level of literacy within marginalised communities is often given as a reason for the failure of community print media to act as a viable medium for marginalised communities. In the past, however, community publications such as *Learn and Teach*, played an important role in improving literacy and could continue to do so in the future. For some organisations working on the ground, the perception persists that the most accessible and desirable form of media remains low tech print media such as T-shirt design production, posters or banner making.

Community video, on the other hand, is deemed too expensive and too skills intensive for the community sector. And yet video is viewed as a powerful medium for education, advocacy and lobbying and as a means of amplifying traditional storytelling and theatre. The absence of an enabling environment has not prevented the proliferation of either which is perhaps the best possible indicator that such a need exists.

The digitisation of media technologies allows for digital audio, video, print and multimedia production on one digital platform. With improvements in audio and video compression and decompression, programme exchange over the Internet could be a reality in the very near future. Indeed, some broadcasters are already doing this with existing bandwidth. The other positive aspect of new media technologies is that they are becoming cheaper and more accessible. Media practitioners are increasingly using the Internet for e-mail, research, discussion groups and information exchange. The transition form broadcasting to bit-casting, while still being some way off, will change the broadcasting environment into an interactive multimedia form of communication.

It is critical that small media, which is emerging on the cusp of these important technological innovations, 'leapfrogs' traditional forms of media and embraces digital technology and its multiple uses. This will, in turn, create the opportunity for small media to 'piggy back' on government efforts to promote an 'information society' through the provision of universal access to ICTs. Improved access to computers through telecentres and MPCCs has created such opportunities.

As a result of these developments, the sector has seen the emergence of innovative multimedia projects providing access to every conceivable combination of computers, radio, video, visual and performing arts and information services – often in the context of youth centres, CACs, MPCCs, telecentres or within a traditional community media centre. Many of these are based in rural areas.

The strategic use of ICTs by small media formations has a number of benefits including networking, research, information and programme exchange. Small media is in a position to access information and repackage it in ways that are more accessible to the community through popular forms of dissemination such as radio and print. Small media also creates a platform for the creation of indigenous local content on the world wide web.

Many NGOs employ cross-media strategies including print, audio-visual and web materials to promote their development and empowerment objectives. In addition to the above, Idasa, Agenda and Workers World Radio (WWR) are now working closely with community broadcasters to develop and distribute radio content. NGO media strategies are generally aimed at marginalised communities or communities of interest and deal with social justice issues such as gender, land rights, sustainable development and the environment. These strategies usually focus on improving networking and information exchange, education, awareness raising campaigns or social marketing. The health sector is probably the most advanced in this respect with many examples of well known, successful projects such as LoveLife, the Media Training Centre (MTC) and Soul City.

It is increasingly clear that the media can no longer be neatly divided into print, radio and audiovisual. A new terminology is starting to emerge to describe this phenomenon, namely, CMS – as it is described by the DoC – and MCCCs, as it is explained by the GCIS. But the synergies do not only exist at the level of technology. The future success of small media rests on its ability to transform into a shared communication vehicle between all community stakeholders including civic structures, NGOs, educational institutions, local business, citizens and government.

Ironically, while we witness the organic emergence of multimedia initiatives, many emerging community radio, audiovisual and print initiatives continue to operate independently from one another. This inevitably leads to a waste of resources and encourages duplication and competition. It also flies in the face of current international trends towards multimedia and convergence.

A groundbreaking conference entitled the Community Electronic Multimedia (CEM) Indaba, held at Helderfontein Estate in Johannesburg in November 2001, aimed at addressing this situation marked a shift in government thinking towards community media services in South Africa. The purpose of the Indaba was to 'deliberate on a strategy for the development a community electronic multimedia sector [which] responds to technological convergence challenges at grassroots level and government's integrated development strategy [and an] urgent need to re-align and integrate our services' (CEM 2001: 8).

The CEM Indaba agreed on the need to develop a comprehensive policy either through new legislation or policy encouraging the integrated governance principle. A CMS TT was mandated to work with the DoC to take this work forward. The report of this team was presented at a follow-up Indaba in November 2003, during which stakeholders were consulted.

According to the GCIS, an expanded concept of multimedia communication centres is aimed at empowering communities by:
- Providing access to information as well as the means to produce and disseminate information;
- Contributing to the development of the community;
- Enhancing and facilitating programmes around education and literacy;
- Job creation; and
- Community cultural development.

CMS places the emphasis on resource sharing (such as a building, connectivity and an administrative core) between related information and communication services at a local level. This results in a diversification of services, thereby increasing income generation opportunities and at the same time reducing costs.

3.6 Conclusion

Ultimately, the guiding principle is that it should be up to the community itself to decide on the appropriate form of communication to meets its needs. This choice is usually determined by:
- The communication and information needs of the community;
- How existing, traditional modes of communication can be complemented;
- The availability of existing local resources (through resource mapping); and
- The outcome of lobbying/partnership-building efforts to tap into these resources (for example, the existing local newspaper may agree to take on trainees from the black community and be more receptive to this community's information needs).

The People's Voice

Unesco's document *Promoting Community Media in Africa* highlights the need for situation-specific research: 'The choice of media is a variable to be determined with the community rather than pre-determined by exogenous interests and priorities' (Opubor 2000: 16). The work stresses that a needs assessment must include what information is needed and what components (of a community communication system) require special help. Although it is true that resources – human, financial and technical – can, and often do, determine the choice of medium for a community media initiative, the nature and purpose of the community media initiatives should be the most important determinants' (Wanyeki 2000: 30).

The case studies conducted by this project showed that not one small media organisation had conducted a communication needs assessment of their community prior to developing plans to set up a radio station or newspaper. Had this been done properly from the outset, the resulting communication plan may well have been different and, in all likelihood, better suited to the immediate needs and capacity of the community.

In the South African context, it is noticeable that objectives with regard to small media opportunities are set very high. Groups waiting for a community radio licence, for instance, often wait for years without initiating simple, cost-effective media-generation activities such as newsletters or community noticeboards. It may be the case that a particular community has priorities other than the establishment of a radio station. Drama, oral poetry or production of educational videos may be more appropriate, depending on identified needs.

Print media skills such as computer literacy, design and editing will certainly come in useful for multimedia or radio production (scriptwriting, for example) but will also provide volunteers and participants with basic, empowering skills for their own development. Even if a community has ambitious goals for a radio station and multimedia facility, incremental steps, perhaps starting with a simple newsletter or noticeboard, may well prove a good starting point which will continue to provide the facility with income, marketing and communication resources and opportunities.

The research carried out in this project has given much greater clarity to the topography of the local media sector, and the service providers who cater to it. There has not been previous work that has presented details of this nature on the size of the sector, the proportion of advertising income, the current status of organisations or on the various initiatives taking place within the sector. In the next chapter the implications of this information is analysed and recommendations are presented on the way forward.

4 ANALYSIS AND CONCLUSIONS

4.1 Introduction

This chapter makes use of the various sources of information and data that were gathered during the course of this project. This includes the extensive case study interviews, the service provider questionnaires, the database, interviews with key funders together with the literature and policy overviews.

The topics covered have been broken down into the most important areas and include HRD, governance, community participation, funding and financial sustainability, content, technology, the roles of the principal players, gender and disability and the accessing of underserviced areas. Various possibilities for further research are also included.

This chapter presents our conclusions to the MDDA as they have emerged out of our research. Some of these conclusions have emanated out of other publications or research, such as from the PDU, the CMS TT or from the IMA, and are included with the intention of giving the MDDA the full picture.

In line with the broad objectives of this report, these conclusions are not necessarily all pertinent to the role and mandate of MDDA but are general suggestions and opinions addressed to the small media sector as a whole. It is not the assumption of the authors that it is incumbent on the MDDA, or indeed part of its legislative mandate, to implement these objectives. Where it is not within the scope of the MDDA to act on conclusions that they subscribe to, it is hoped that the MDDA will use its considerable leverage to influence developments in line with such conclusions. Finally, these are the authors' conclusions and are not intended to reflect the views of the MDDA.

Conclusion 1: Targeting least-serviced areas and groups
It is no great surprise to see that small media organisations are overly focused in the urban areas, particularly in the main metropolitan centres, and in the wealthiest provinces. (See Figures 1 to 4.) While the overwhelming urban bias is perhaps expected, the distortions in provincial distribution are more surprising, given the objective of small media to communicate predominantly with those who don't have access to the mainstream media.

There tends to be an over-concentration of media in more developed provinces and urban centres with blind spots in the most underdeveloped rural communities with no clear development strategy to extend the roll-out of information and communications services to these areas.

In addition, while our research shows a reasonable level of gender awareness and opportunities for the disabled among service providers, this is a serious problem among small media organisations themselves. We found that while women, in particular, were popular audiences for local media products, representivity within the media organisations and their boards was often very poor.

When it comes to making decisions on funding allocations, the MDDA should naturally give priority to least-served areas and groups, while at the same time consolidating services in existing areas. It is vital to note, however, that international best practice and the evidence of our own case studies clearly indicate that fundamental to the success of any local media initiative is the drive, will and the commitment of a small group of

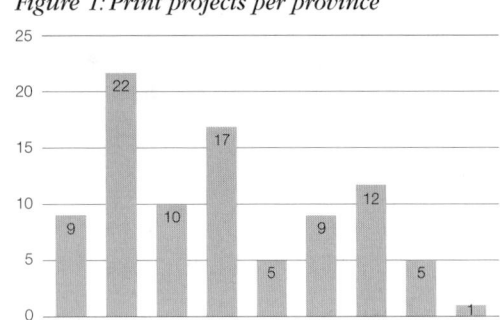

Figure 1: Print projects per province

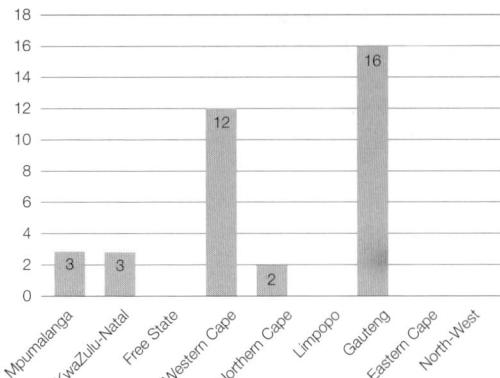

Figure 2: Service provider projects per province

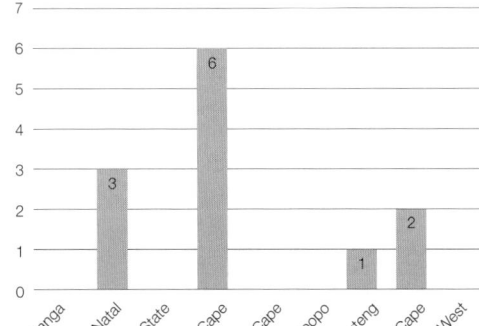

Figure 3: Multimedia projects per province

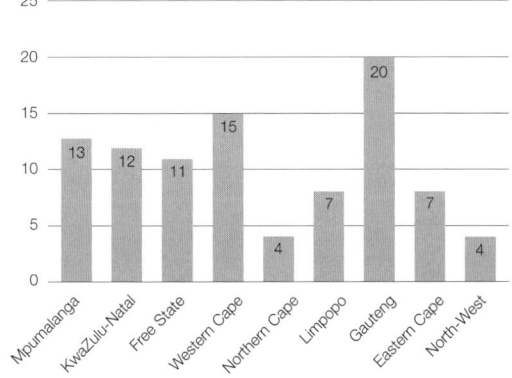

Figure 4: Radio projects per province

individuals at a local level. People are the key ingredient for success – locals who identify a need and who are willing to fight for it. This is a fundamental sustainability factor. It is not appropriate therefore to suggest that the MDDA should identify underserviced areas and somehow initiate, suggest or introduce media to these areas. This has to be largely a bottom up process (see Conclusion 2). The MDDA should learn from the mistakes of DACST (now DAC and DST), USA and the GCIS who have been accused (Hagg 2002, Benjamin 2001) of creating 'white elephants' in the form of CACs, telecentres and MPCCs respectively. In order to assist with the process of identifying need, we urge the following:

Conclusion 2: National awareness campaign
Many people are not aware of the importance and relevance of small media and the role it can play in their community. In order to deal with this problem it is suggested that the MDDA embark on a national awareness campaign. Such a campaign need not be conducted in isolation from other efforts to promote media education for South African citizens. A similar initiative is already underway under the banner of the NMEI, involving a wide range of organisations including the Film and Publications Board (who initiated it), the SABC, the NFVF, academic institutions, the DoE, organised business and NGOs. The NMEI Task Team is in the process of developing a two-pronged strategy targeting schools on one hand (and envisaging the development of media education in schools) and the general population on the other. This latter dimension includes a national media awareness campaign, including newspaper coverage, media educational programming on national television and a range of other ideas.

ANALYSIS AND CONCLUSIONS

Conclusion 3: Complete the mapping process
This project has mapped the coverage of community and independent media through a database and mapping exercise. While this gives a good idea of the distribution of local media in South Africa, it would certainly be useful for the MDDA to cross-reference this map with the penetration of public and commercial media. It is important that the SABC be called on to assist with providing its own penetration statistics, but it was not possible, in the scope and timeframe of this research project, to include this or other mapping elements. The combination of the three mapping exercises would clearly identify the country's most critically underserviced areas.

The MDDA may wish to send a 'roadshow' to those areas or use its leverage to persuade existing service providers to focus on these. It might be useful to develop a grading system, to assist in differentiating between most-serviced and least-serviced areas, such as:
- Grade A: Areas where there is no media coverage (including public and private);
- Grade B: Areas serviced by SABC radio only;
- Grade C: Areas covered by SABC radio and television;
- Grade D: Areas covered by SABC radio, television and commercial publishers;
- Grade E: Areas already served by local media and needing financial support; and
- Grade F: Areas served by local media needing no financial support but seeking to benefit from support, such as information and networking.

Conclusion 4: Merge and collaborate
Research has shown that in some areas more than one community media project exists, often competing for limited resources and not co-operating with each other. It is the assumption of the authors that competitiveness is not a value that should be over-emphasised in the community media sector. Where more than one community media initiative (including a telecentre) exists in an area, these should be encouraged to merge. In areas where there is both a community and an independent media organisation, these should be encouraged to collaborate closely.

The same would apply to the duplication of services offered by service providers (please refer to Conclusion 6 under Human Resource Development).

Conclusion 5: Target existing building blocks
In line with the thinking of the CMS Task Team, existing community structures such as MPCCs, youth centres, CACs, telecentres and other organisations working with youth, information and development services (such as 'advice offices') are ideal building blocks for community media services. Once underserviced areas have been identified, the MDDA may wish to target these for their 'awareness raising' interventions.

The DAC is currently undertaking an audit of CACs and science centres. The Universal Service Agency should have an updated database of telecentres and the GCIS a full list of MPCCs. Civil society formations should also be targeted, through structures such as the CBO network, South African National Civics Organisation (SANCO) and the South African NGO Coalition.

> **A note on sustainability**
>
> In noting the 'growing phenomenon' of community media in Africa, Unesco experts have warned that 'many of the existing and emerging community media do not possess the economic, technical and human resources required for sustainability' (Boafo 2000: 5). Reflecting this sentiment, almost all of our 25 case studies reported they were either struggling to survive or were barely covering costs. None of the case studies indicated they had reached a position of profitability.
>
> For the PDU, a sustainable publisher is one that 'generates profit, ploughs back working capital, pays salaries, grows its human resources and innovates technically so it can add value to society'. In other words, it simply demonstrates 'the ability to stay in business and provide ongoing, valuable spin-offs to the community' (PDU 2002: 12).
>
> It is our contention that sustainability is not just about financial arrangements. As Hagg has argued, sustainability is a highly complex and multi-sectoral issue, involving legislative and legal frameworks, funding, skills, support and a continuous rebuilding process (Hagg 2002: 19).
>
> It is this broad notion of sustainability that lies at the heart of this research and is the principal motive for the questions directed to community media managers: what is it that needs to be done to create an enabling environment in which the local media sector can flourish?

The key question of sustainability will be dealt with in the rest of this chapter under the following headings:
- Human resource development
- Institutional capacity building
- Partnerships
- Financial modelling
- Networking and information
- Content development
- Technical sustainability

4.2 Human resource development

The small media sector is served by at least 19 training service providers, most of which are based in the urban centres with an especially heavy weighting in the Western Cape and Gauteng. Most of the training providers surveyed have mobile training or outreach facilities and/or train nationally. They are largely non-profit organisations and offer high quality, large-scale services to a broad diversity of organisations.

Many of the 19 participating training service providers caters for different sectors simultaneously with 17 indicating that they provide services to the radio sector, 14 to the video sector, 9 to multimedia and the visual arts, 6 to the design sector and 3 provide technical support or cater for the performing arts.

Table 1 breaks this information down further.

Analysis and conclusions

Table 1: Breakdown of 19 participating training service providers

Location	Name	Reach	Primary focus
Durban	Agenda	National	Print, radio – gender focus
	Vuleka	National	Video, radio
Cape Town	BTI	SADC region	Radio
	Mediaworks	N, W & E Cape	Print, multimedia
	Idasa	National	Radio – democracy, human rights
	CVET	Mainly local	Video
	MTC	National	Radio, print, multimedia – health
	Globecom	National	Radio, video – technical services
	WMW	SADC region	Gender advocacy
	Centre for the Book	National	Print
Johannesburg	IAJ	National	Radio, print
	Nemisa	National	Radio, video, multimedia
	NFTS	National	Video
	Gender Link	SADC region	Gender advocacy
	ABC Ulwazi	National	Radio
	FRU	National	Video Resource Centres
	MMP	National	Media monitoring
	PictureNET	National, International	Photographic scanning
Victoria West	Apollo	Local, province	Video, ICTs

The case studies confirmed the following:
- The services offered by training service providers are considered average to good (by the 25 case study participants) indicating that there are certainly enough qualified and knowledgeable people in the sector to make a real impact on the future of community media. But the quality of training, although generally regarded as average to good, is uneven.
- Besides what is happening at the level of the NQF there is little happening in the way of standards-setting or quality control.
- Major problems have been identified with regards to the co-ordination of training leading to duplication, competition and gaps in training. While there is clearly collaboration happening in the sector, this tends to be ad hoc.
- All the case study interviewees indicated they wanted training conducted in their home province and preferably on-site. There was also a desire for sharing experiences and resources at a sub-regional level.
- Training is required for board members as well as for volunteers, in particular regarding their roles within a community media organisation.

THE PEOPLE'S VOICE

- Training for the trainers is also needed. Numeracy skills are lacking, which inhibits organisations' capacity to produce funding applications as well as market and/or audience research.
- Virtually no organisation is tapping into corporate social investment (sponsorship), which implies that training is also needed in this area.
- Project management, including managing partnerships, is an important training area, given the importance of partnership and collaboration for the sector.

The case studies listed an extremely broad range of training needs. Not surprisingly, the three of the most frequent requests were all related to financial sustainability. These were: financial management, fundraising and marketing. Other sought-after training areas were communication skills, education on the role of media in development, media law, communication skills, writing skills and journalism skills. Completing the 'top ten' are media literacy, radio production and conflict resolution skills (see below).

4.2.1 Lessons from the radio sector

Until 2000, the NCRF was both a player and a referee when it came to training for the community radio sector, both conducting and co-ordinating training. Since then, the NCRF has limited its role to co-ordination and has undertaken several studies in the last few years in order to develop a clear strategy for training service provision, including:

- 1997–2001 Community Radio Training Evaluation (Nell and Shapiro 2001); and
- Training Plan for the period September 2001–February 2004 by Succinct (taking forward recommendations from the evaluation).

With some assistance from the MAPPP SETA, the organisation Succinct undertook:
- An assessment of training needs;
- An audit of service providers and who is providing what; and
- A development of a training plan.

This plan, to be implemented between September 2001 and February 2004, envisaged:
- The development of one skilled trainer in every radio station, whose core function would be to transfer skills to others. This would be achieved by:
  - Knowledge transfer;
  - Designing and implementing basic programmes;
  - Assessing skills against agreed outcomes and assessment criteria; and
  - Using the 'hub model' to further share knowledge and resources with other regional trainers.

A training plan (see below) was structured to deliver high priority training areas first. Each training block was to consist of eight sessions, spread out over two months, made up of 15 delegates and clustered around geographical areas. Each training session would be followed by an assessment and the training plan would be reviewed once a year.

High priority (to be delivered in all nine provinces in year one):
- Using radio as a community development tool (two days);
- Train the trainer (five days);
- Computer literacy (one day);
- Radio programming (two days);
- Station management (three days);

Analysis and conclusions

- Financial management (duration not given);
- Advertising and marketing (two days); and
- Newsroom (one day).

Medium priority:
- Governance;
- Communication skills;
- Presentation skills;
- Projection and use of voice;
- Technical equipment;
- Sound and audio engineering; and
- Information Technology (IT) skills.

Low priority:
- Audience analysis and education;
- Computer skills – Internet;
- Research skills;
- Library management;
- Coaching and mentoring;
- Editing – text; and
- Fundraising.

This plan is aimed at dealing with the training needs of the community radio sector. Yet it is clear from our research that the training needs of print, audiovisual and multimedia projects are very similar. This plan was never implemented due to capacity problems in the national office of the NCRF. In the meantime, service providers continue to operate independently. According to one NCRF member interviewed during the course of this project: 'Training continues to be donor driven, with little regard to the training needs of stations. People are tired of going to training which does not meet their needs'.

A (training) Providers Forum was established in August 2001 as a loose network of providers to assist the NCRF in fulfilling its mandate to develop the sector. It was not intended to duplicate the work of the SGB of the NQF. The role of the forum is to ensure:
- Co-ordination;
- Information sharing; and
- Joint planning (for example, regarding the Sector Skills Plan).

Providers made a commitment to work in the following areas:
- Train the trainer;
- Networking with station-based trainers;
- Creation of internships;
- Liaison with the industry; and
- Encouraging of partnerships and specialisation.

The Providers Forum reconvened in early 2003, where similar concerns were raised. In the meantime, training co-ordination seems to have migrated to the provincial hubs. It is through these 'hubs' that stations come together to support one another and collaborate around marketing, training, station management, gender and programming.

The people's voice

In terms of the sector's interaction with the NQF, the community radio sector is represented on the Media Advisory Committee (MAC) of the MAPPP SETA. In addition, the sector is contributing to unit standards in the Audiovisual Production SGB and the Journalism SGB. Approximately half of the training providers are in the process of seeking accreditation with MAPPP SETA.

The NCRF has developed a Procurement Policy for procuring training services.

4.2.2 Training for print

On the print side, the PDU and the Sanef are the only organisations with recently documented experience from which to draw.

The PDU identified four broad areas of skills development, namely:
- Financial and management systems;
- Advertising and marketing;
- Editorial and design; and
- IT – this training was never implemented due to ongoing technical capacity problems amongst most local publishers.

Training interventions by the PDU took the form of a number of on-site visits, including needs assessments, staff training, target setting, monitoring and mentoring. In addition, staff were encouraged to attend a central training programme, consisting of short courses, offered by the PDU in Johannesburg.

The completion in 2002 of a skills audit commissioned by Sanef provides an important backdrop to the small media sector's skills levels. At Sanef's AGM in 2000, which led to the audit, it was agreed that improving the quality of journalism was the major challenge facing the South African media industry. The audit found skills levels were worse than expected. On the positive side, a new level of commitment to ongoing training and education has been articulated by top management within the mainstream media sector (Tsedu, Wrotlesley & Clay 2002: 5).

Among the important recommendations emanating out of the Sanef report were: urgent attention to reporting, writing and accuracy skills; improved interaction between the media and training institutions; and greater haste toward designing and implementing a regulated system of internship and accreditation. In the opinion of the reporters surveyed in the audit, the top four ranking skills most desired were: newsgathering skills (accuracy, angles, beats, contacts, reporting, interviewing), conceptual skills (analysis, creativity, general knowledge, narrative) and writing skills and practical skills. The Sanef skills audit recommendations also called for a renewed emphasis on 'life skills' and critical reflectiveness (Tsedu et al. 2002: 5).

Conclusion 6: Developing an integrated HRD plan
The MDDA should work in close consultation with the networks to develop and implement an integrated human resources development plan for the small media sector. Serious consideration should be given to whether this should incorporate the training needs of radio, print and audiovisual media or whether these sectors should be dealt with separately. This decision should take into account the most pressing training needs across

Analysis and conclusions

the whole sector, the fact that most service providers work in more than one form of media, and the realities of convergence.

Key stakeholders who should be involved in developing such a plan include:
- The NFVF;
- The Universal Service Agency (USA);
- Nemisa;
- MAPPP SETA;
- Training service providers including higher education institutions; and
- Networks.

Much work has and is being done to see to the training needs of community and independent media, on the one hand, and for the mainstream industry, on the other. What is now needed is an overarching, integrated strategy, which explores synergies and overlaps to ensure that we don't 'ghetto-ise' community media training. Such a strategy should outline a landscape for training, perhaps including the following levels:
- Media education for citizens – perhaps through the schooling system;
- Community-based, entry-level skills programmes that are work-based, which could act as a bridging level between school and higher education (such as those provided by local media);
- Provincial media access centres or service providers acting as 'development hubs' for the development of local media;
- Higher educational institutions – perhaps working to build education capacity at all other levels; and
- A national film school.

It is not unthinkable to envisage a partial restructuring of service delivery to ensure geographic diversity. This would envisage the voluntary merging of providers in urban centres and the creation of new ones in under-serviced areas.

Conclusion 7: Learning from previous training experiences
This plan should take cognisance of the lessons learned over the past decade of training. These lessons include:
- New, emerging projects should undergo a participatory research process to identify their communications needs and develop a communications plan.
- This should include an organisational development process during which a business plan is developed. At this point, a needs assessment should be conducted, including a technical assessment. This is the plan against which future training interventions will be measured.
- Training interventions should be split between on-site mentorship and clustered training.
- Training should cater for new entrants as well as the needs of more established organisations.
- Different training interventions should be targeted at different functions within the media organisation. With small media organisations this can usually be broken down into management/financial/governance functions (director) and content/technical related functions (Programme Manager/trainer). It is particularly important that the latter be accompanied by a 'train the trainer' course, as this is the person most likely to be transferring skills to many other volunteers/interns.

THE PEOPLE'S VOICE

- Where possible training should be clustered regionally (provincially). This will also serve to improve networking and co-ordination on a regional level.
- Training components should be structured to last between two to five days.
- Training should take place no less than two months apart, giving people time to run their organisations.
- Training providers need to be encouraged to develop their own areas of specialisation and work collaboratively.
- In order to raise the general level of training provision it may be necessary to facilitate a process whereby training providers come together and share training curricula and materials and transfer skills ('train the trainer').
- All training interventions should be accompanied by the production and distribution of user-friendly training manuals, translated into other languages, to encourage a multiplier effect – particularly in light of the 'train the trainer' approach.
- Exchanges between local media organisations and between local and mainstream media are valuable.

Conclusion 8: Piloting skills learnerships
Apart from its contribution to the work of the SGBs, it is suggested that the community media sector consider following the example of the creative industries, through Create SA and MAPPP SETA, and pilot skills programmes or learnerships in community media theory and practice. This could be offered at Level 4 with electives in video, radio, print and multimedia. This should not seek to duplicate the work of the SGBs but rather seek to draw on existing unit standards, with a view to customising a qualification around the needs of small media. This project could be implemented as a collaboration between service providers who are willing to share and strengthen their respective curricula and training materials. Higher education institutions could also be drawn in to tap their expertise.

During this process, different service providers should agree on their particular areas of specialisation and concentrate on these. The learnership or skills programme would then be registered with SAQA for accreditation and piloted through the various service providers. In the process, service providers and trainers would be accredited. Learnerships should be targeted initially at trainers within the small media sector, leading to a trickle down effect whereby small media organisations are themselves providing accredited work-based skills programmes to volunteer/interns (refer to 'Managing volunteers' below for more details).

Conclusion 9: Clarification of the MDDA's role
It is critical for the MDDA to set out its role clearly in relation to that of the networks and the service providers. This should be understood by all and communicated unambiguously. It is vital that the MDDA taps into existing expertise in the sector and does not duplicate the work that the service providers are already doing. The MDDA needs to enable the network to play its role effectively, use its leverage to raise the standard of training, press service providers to work together and focus on the gaps in service provision.

Conclusion 10: Understanding the role of 'hubs'
The role of provincial hubs has been highlighted elsewhere, notably:
- In a paper, Towards Optimally Functioning Community Arts Centres, in which 'centres of excellence' are identified as playing an important role in capacity building for smaller, emerging centres (Hagg 2002).

Analysis and conclusions

- The NCRF's hub plan through which stations come together at a provincial level to work together on marketing, training co-ordination, gender capacity building.
- The South African Broadcast Production Advisory Bodies' report to the Minister of Communication, which talks about the need for Provincial Multimedia Access Centres acting as 'hubs', for the development of smaller centres and SMME's in each province. It is further suggested that these hubs tap into existing and underutilised resources such as those of the former TBVC broadcasters, higher education institutions, the military and underutilised public buildings; and
- The GCIS speaks about a nodal development approach whereby:
  - Provincial hubs act as a MCCC to the local community; and
  - Rural outreach programmes, aimed at developing smaller, newer centres operate in rural areas.

Clearly, somewhere between these proposals lies a role for provincial networks in collaboration with larger 'centres of excellence' or service providers based in the provinces.

4.3 Institutional capacity building

4.3.1 Managing volunteers

The case studies illustrated the great need for help with the management of volunteers. There appeared to be considerable confusion over the role and reward/incentive system for the volunteers. There have been instances where stations, 'especially those in rural or peri-urban areas, that have as many as 24 or more such "volunteers" at a time, are all getting a cut of the income of the station' (Emdon 2002: 75). One of the dangers of allowing a large number of poorly managed volunteers to be present at small media sites is the potential for the abuse of the telephones. This naturally impacts negatively on sustainability: 'Tough action [is needed] to make every person accountable for business calls and disallow personal calls' (Emdon 2002: 77).

During the research conducted by this project, small media organisations frequently complained of high staff and volunteer turnover rates. Just as volunteers had received their full quota of skills, they acquired jobs often in the formal sector and moved on. While the inconvenience can be appreciated, the transfer of skills and opportunities for employment serve to highlight the important developmental impact of the sector.

The provision of adult basic education and training (ABET) is a vital element of economic empowerment. It is a 'service' that also requires the local media to be more diligent about encouraging the 'each one-teach one' dictum that, in turn, will prevent volunteer turnover from dismantling the capacity of their organisations. Volunteers are available and willing, but it is inevitable that they will be looking for jobs.

Several of the case study interviewees worried about their inability to pay volunteers, were unable to differentiate between different categories of volunteer and had no plan in place for the management of volunteers. Help is certainly required in this area, for instance in the provision of template contracts, the outlining of available incentives and in the delineation of different models of volunteer participation to allow for the different categories of volunteer. These categories could include:
- Some volunteers (let's call them 'rights volunteers' as they are acting on their right to communicate and to access information) have no wish to acquire skills but merely

want to be heard. They should be encouraged to do this, even if it's on a once-off basis.
- Other volunteers (structured intern volunteers) view their participation as a full-time endeavour being the first step toward finding employment or gaining valuable skills. Small media could position itself to provide structured, accredited, work-based skills development linked to placement opportunities for 'graduates' in the private or public sector (especially to local/provincial newspapers or broadcasters) and further training referrals.
- Other volunteers contribute to the running of the organisation by helping with a range of activities including sitting in reception, cleaning floors or helping with basic maintenance. One interesting, and apparently successful model (implemented at the Alexsan Centre in Gauteng) for creating incentives for these volunteers is that for every hour of volunteer support, an hour is earned on the computer, Internet or learning other media-related skills.

It was apparent to the researchers that limits need to be set on the number of structured intern volunteers, perhaps through selection criteria, who can be accommodated in a formal, outcomes-based programme. Access needs to be extended to members of the audience or community who merely have something to say (rights volunteers). This should include both citizens and NGOs/CBOs.

4.3.2 Governance

Just as there was confusion surrounding the role and management of the volunteers, there also appears to be conflicting attitudes concerning the role and composition of the boards governing the community media organisations. Of the 25 case studies that participated in this research, 19 agreed that training should be extended to board members as well as to staff. Due to the high turnover of board members, the role of board development should fall to a particular staff member.

The case studies indicated that problems of interference by board members were common. Board members were frequently under the misapprehension that they are required to exert hands-on authority on community media organisations. This has led to conflict and confusion. Interference by boards in the day-to-day running of community media organisations also has a tendency to introduce local politics (and the tensions and divisions associated with this) into the organisation's work and functioning. The literature confirms that community media are 'integral components of the community that tend to reflect both the agenda and the tactics of the local power structure' (Hindman 1996: 708). A quarter of the case studies reported that the local political environment was having a 'negative impact' on their work. While this may or may not be as a result of the board's interventions, it is a reminder that boards need to be a blend of community representation and expertise.

4.3.3 Staff capacity

In similar fashion, staff members too require clarity on their roles within community media organisations. There needs to be a clear difference between core staff (which should be kept to a minimum) and volunteers. Frequently unpaid or underpaid, staffers need to be assigned contracts and performance goals and also to be incorporated into the strategic planning of the organisation. Many traditional staff roles can be assigned to volunteers to keep down overheads.

ANALYSIS AND CONCLUSIONS

'The more successfully run stations have one or two strong individuals, or a three to four person management team, mandated by the community structures, through a board, to take control and be accountable' (Emdon 2002: 86). The CMS Task Team concurs with this, suggesting that for CMS to be sustainable, it needs a small core of skilled and committed staff, offset by contributions from volunteers from the community. Key positions could include a full-time, skilled director and a programme manager, responsible for training volunteers and programme content.

As the station grows and diversifies its services, it may be necessary to appoint an administrator and a business manager. This suggestion also dovetails with what the NCRF Sector Skill Plan suggests with regards to investing skills in one person in a station who, in turn, passes these skills to others. The authors suggest that, where possible, this should be extended to two people. In terms of skills transfer, the programme manager should develop a structured skills development programme for a manageable number of volunteers and the director should be responsible for staff coaching, mentorship, board development, community outreach and education.

4.3.4 Community access and participation

Of the 25 case studies, a large proportion agreed that they had adopted a wide focus approach to their audiences. Most (20) said they appealed to the 'general population', while women, the youth and church-goers were the most common audiences. The least targeted groups included trade unions, farm workers and NGOs.

Perhaps surprisingly, there appears to be little interaction between community media organisations and local NGOs. This seems a wasted opportunity (and indeed a waived right) to source informed and interested inputs on matters of local importance from the NGO sector. There is even a strong argument suggesting NGOs have a right to (free) access to the community media sector. Public access, the argument goes, does not refer merely to individuals but to all sectors and stakeholders within the community. Certainly the relationship requires investigation and clarification, to the potentially significant benefit of both parties.

It is clear that small media organisations conduct very little research on the communication needs of the communities they serve. Of the 25 case studies, 14 said they had not done participatory research of any kind. International best practice indicates that an assessment of community communication needs is an essential pre-requisite for the establishment and sustainability of a small media operation.

The broad definition of audiences, however, means communities are principally being defined as geographic entities and anyone who tunes in or who is handed a pamphlet or newsletter, counts as a member of the audience. With such wide scope, this naturally presents difficulties in facilitating access. Questions arise as to which segment of large, geographic communities are really being afforded access to the means of media production.

The case studies generally indicate that even where communities have a high level of involvement in the management and ownership of media organisations, access to programming and content provision remain low. In the radio sector, talk shows are largely considered a sufficient vehicle of community participation when combined with the election of board members and popular participation at meetings or AGMs. In some cases, media producers specifically set out to undermine popular attitudes they regard as inappropriate or morally ambivalent. One radio station, for instance, told case study interviewers it was determined to 'challenge [the] contemporary culture' of the youth and re-introduce 'traditional family values'.

Conclusion 11: Establishment of a 'Management Service'
In the authors' opinion, the MDDA should facilitate the establishment of a 'Joint Service Bureau' (as it is called by the IMA) or 'Management Service' (as the PDU referred to it) to facilitate institutional support and development for small media. Assistance could be provided by such a service in the following areas:
- Registrations and legalities;
- Strategy and planning;
- Structure and functions (staff, volunteers and board);
- Human resource policies;
- Loan applications;
- Financial administration and management;
- Taxation;
- Administration;
- Copy editing;
- Organisational practice;
- Research methodology; and
- A handbook on managing volunteers.

Conclusion 12: Resource manual and/or website
The above 'agency' should be developed in conjunction with resource materials available in a file, for constant updating, and a website which is easy to navigate and has a range of useful materials that can be downloaded on request. This might include human resource policies, contract templates and form letters for business transactions, legal documents, registration forms, examples of advertising rate cards, training materials and links to important sights such as SAQA and MAPPP SETA. There are small media organisations who perform this kind of work and who should be allowed to tender for it.

4.3.5 Ownership structure

It is currently in the mandate of the MDDA to support community and independent media. However, it is important to note that many NGOs produce media and have a serious claim to be considered part of, as well as providing services to, the local media sector. Armed with capacity, producing a significant output of media products and already representing more than a third of the budgetary value of the sector, these NGOs occupy an important position. The MDDA should not discount community media that function as service organisations and that have other ways of facilitating community participation, such as through research.

The Community Multimedia Services Task Team discussed some of the advantages and disadvantages of the following legal/ownership models for community multimedia services (CMS TT Draft report 2003):
- Entrepreneurial model;
- Community (ownership and control) based organisation (CBO);
- NGO service organisation model; and
- Facilities management model.

Analysis and conclusions

In the final analysis, the task team felt that the ideal model was one that takes in the best elements of all four, including:
- A balance between service delivery and cost recovery;
- Community ownership and control;
- Clear accountability;
- Sound business practice;
- A governance structure that allows for energy, innovation, entrepreneurial incentives, initiative;
- Community access and participation;
- Understanding of and responsiveness to community needs;
- Stable, medium sized organisation with capacity and resources to deliver quality services;
- Organisational excellence;
- A mixed economy, based on a diversification of services, including cost recovery and funded activities; and
- Cost effectiveness and resource sharing.

Conclusion 13: Local media models
In the authors' opinion, the MDDA should avoid a normative approach in which it seeks to impose a particular 'model' for small media. A project need not be judged on its ownership structure but on the quality of its service delivery to the user group.

4.4 Partnerships

Partnerships are probably one of the most critical and yet least appreciated elements of sustainability. Arguably, the future success of small media rests on its ability to identify and form partnerships with entities that contribute resources and capacity.

From the analysis of the case studies, it can be concluded that the establishment and management of partnerships (such as those with schools and/or businesses), has been a weakness in the sector, with the exception of the service providers. However, very few formal links exist between the training service providers and higher educational institutions, in spite of the obvious overlap in interests and services. Assistance with the identification of potential partnerships and help with partnership management is sorely needed.

According to the CMS Task Team, the need for partnerships is informed by three key considerations:
- Technical convergence: Technological innovations such as digitisation are creating opportunities for all forms of media to be produced across one digital platform.
- Infrastructure and economic considerations: Combined infrastructure between related services reduces costs and encouraged collaboration.
- Social development considerations: The process of building partnerships between CBOs, NGOs, business and local authorities with the aim of creating a shared communications channel is crucial to the success of CMS (Scott 1996).

The process of identifying partnerships should start at the outset during the participatory research or media planning phase.

Resource mapping is a useful exercise in order to identify existing resources that may be harnessed to achieve a community's communication goals. Through this process the community may identify synergies with similar structures such as:
- A MPCC, CAC, youth centre or other building in which the project could be housed; and
- A local telecentre or schoolsnet facility through which access to computers can be secured.

In addition to these synergistic institutional arrangements, the media initiative may identify a range of stakeholders, all of whom stand to benefit from media services and who may also have something to contribute towards the initiative. For example,
- Civil society organisations and citizens:
  Give: volunteers' efforts;
  Get: access to information and communication, skills development opportunities.
- Government:
  Give: office space, access to facilities, communications contracts;
  Get: communication services.
- Local business:
  Give: advertising contracts, payment for use of services;
  Get: access to a wider market for their goods and services, access to business services (photocopying, design services, etc.), access to skilled volunteers.

4.4.1 Community multimedia services

The notion of multistakeholder partnerships lies at the heart of CMS. The CMS Task Team has defined CMS as 'an integrated communication and information service designed to meet the cultural, social and economic needs of a geographical community or a community of interest' (CMS Task Team Report 2003: 1). The GCIS, referring to 'Multimedia Community Communications Centres (MCCCs) points out that 'the motivation for partnerships for community and media development is intended to enable the leveraging of existing resources, where possible, thereby ensuring proper co-ordination of activities to maximise the use of resources and prevent duplication' (GCIS 2002: 4).

Benjamin's research on telecentres has shown that successful telecentres are ones that have managed to focus on content and have established ties with local media structures. Telecentres on their own are not viable (Benjamin 2001: 68).

This notion of CMS as a shared, information and communication vehicle has two main benefits:
- Economies of scale: CMS reduces costs, encourages the best utilisation of limited local resources and taps into 'in-kind' contributions. Resource sharing includes tariffs, connectivity, one 'pipeline' and infrastructure.
- It allows community media to diversify its services and therefore its sources of income (refer to 'Financial modelling' on p.84 for details).

Conclusion 14: Convergence
The MDDA should give serious consideration to the impact of convergence on the future of small media including the emergence of CMS. This may have serious implications for the strategies adopted by the agency as well as the funding criteria, priorities and indeed

Analysis and conclusions

structure of the MDDA. The MDDA needs to create an enabling and encouraging environment for the emergence of CMS.

4.4.2 Small media and the role of government

There is no question that government has an important role within the small media sector. A partnership between local media and government should, however, be discussed on two levels:
- Various government or statutory bodies provide funding and other support to local media such as the MDDA, the DoC, the NFVF, the Universal Service Agency, local government, social services and the National Arts Council (this will be dealt with in more detail under 'Financial modelling'). This funding is underpinned by specific national policy directives aimed at promoting redress and diversity in the media.
- On the other hand, there is a client/service relationship between government and small media whereby it can act as an important vehicle of communication and information between the government and the people. In this way the argument for a partnership with government goes beyond pleas for government hand-outs towards a mutually beneficial relationship whereby government gets something back for its financial contribution.

The role of government is crucial to the development and sustainability of the small media sector in South Africa. The case study data indicates that a high proportion of small media organisations have signed formal agreements with one or another government department or agency. Among the case studies alone, the DoC, housing, social services, local government, offices of premiers and the GCIS were all formally involved with the sector.

The GCIS has a formal relationship with the community radio sector through which it broadcasts government information in exchange for a fee. This is already having a marked and positive impact on stations income. The IMA, on the other hand, has expressed frustration, on behalf of its 78 members, about the lack of information about where and how to access government information. The IMA has called for a resource manual to facilitate access by small publishers to government. This appears to the authors of this report to be a good idea.

In spite of this variety of support, none of the organisations reported a satisfactory situation had been achieved in which their needs or expectations were being met by government. In some cases, the political nature of the governmental interventions proved to be seriously debilitating. Some small media organisations function as little more than government communication instruments taking all their content from government and relying on government for editorial direction and financial security. One organisation operated entirely out of a premier's office. This, naturally, undermines the independence and credibility of media organisations. It also makes them vulnerable not necessarily to government as a whole but to particular officials with personal ambitions and objectives. Bear in mind, too, that national elections tend to increase pressure on small media to embrace dominant local loyalties. (It should be noted that as well as a threat, the national election of 2004 also presents an excellent opportunity for strengthening the community media sector. This should be pursued by the MDDA.)

It is clear that there is little understanding within the various government departments of a uniform attitude or policy with regard to the handling of the small media sector. This gives those organisations no tangible defence against interfering officials. Many of the small media organisations reported the presence of government members on their governing boards. This makes the importance of clarifying guidelines all the more important.

There is no doubt that government is an important ally to the sector and there is great potential for assistance. One way in which government could help is in alleviating the high cost of office rental that cripples so many community media organisations. Surely government can assist small media organisations with access to free or low cost office space?

In situations where local and provincial government structures themselves suffer from a lack of capacity, it is not surprising that many found it hard to connect with development initiatives or tap into formal funding channels. Just over half of the case studies (13) reported no involvement in – or even knowledge of – local IDP processes. This was a trend that mirrored the CAC sector which also reported low levels of involvement in the IDP. Research suggested that among the CACs, 'few managers seemed to know about the requirements for IDP participation (nor did they realise) it is compulsory for any council to include all publicly-funded activities in the IDP' (Hagg 2002: 27).

Conclusion 15: Government-local media relations
On the subject of the relationship between government and local media, the authors' recommend the following conclusions are considered by the MDDA:
- The MDDA should raise awareness within government about the benefits of using local media as a vehicle for government information and within the small media about the role of small media in promoting participatory democracy and sustainable development.
- The MDDA should facilitate the production of a resource manual to facilitate access by small media to government and access by government to local media outlets.
- The MDDA should lobby government to encourage relevant government departments to make facilities available to local media such as shared infrastructure and office space.
- The MDDA should facilitate a Code of Practice, similar to the one recommended by the media industry to guide and clarify the relationship between small media and government. The MDDA also needs to look into the kind of information being disseminated by government through the small media sector and, in consultation with government and the sector, set appropriate guidelines for what is permissible and what is not. This could include the design and distribution of policy guidelines, including information on editorial independence and media ethics. Collaboration with other industry bodies, including Sanef, is urged in designing this Code of Practice.

One of the main factors inhibiting the use of small media structures by government, is that, like advertisers, government wants value for money in terms of reaching as wide an audience as possible.

ANALYSIS AND CONCLUSIONS

Conclusion 16: Marketing procurement agency
It is the opinion of the authors that the MDDA should, in partnership with the networks, explore the establishment of a national and/or marketing procurement agency to facilitate access by small media to government communications contracts. This could be linked to the Advertising Procurement Agency (APA) dealt with under 'Financial Modelling' (Conclusion 22 on p.92).

4.4.3 Partnership with the mainstream media

In the ten years since the advent of democracy in South Africa, the media sector has achieved a greater degree of diversity but it remains far short of what is possible or even necessary. It is now a common assumption, both in South Africa and abroad, that the marketplace occupied by the mainstream media is far from sufficient as an engine for the generation of media diversity.

There has been little change in the concentration of media ownership in South Africa in the last ten years, though the locale or pattern of ownership has shifted. As media analyst Sean Jacobs argues: 'State-sponsored or market-led changes … have not on the whole resulted in the expected opening up of the media. In fact, the public sphere remains in many ways the same: reflecting the same inequalities of access as well as power, and also introducing new ones as media changes coincide with the narrow political and economic transition that is currently unfolding in South Africa' (Jacobs 2003: 7).

And, just as changes in patterns of ownership have failed to impact substantively on media diversity, so relations between the small media sector and the mainstream industry continue to be uneven. One analyst of community media in the Caribbean noted that the mainstream commercial media in his part of the world 'continue to harbour negative feelings about community media and are convinced of their own ability to adequately serve community needs' (Cholmondeley 2000: 100). The authors suspect the situation in South Africa is not entirely dissimilar.

There is no question that a degree of discomfort against a background of vague disinterest characterises the media industry's attitude toward the community media sector. One organisation, the Community Print Association (CPA), does attempt to bring the mainstream and independent community print media together. At the time of going to press, the CPA was experiencing grave difficulties and its future was in doubt. Many of the mainstream media corporations operate their own 'community organs' in the form of knock-and-drop newspapers or house commercial publishing divisions while the SABC still has control over a large number of radio stations servicing different communities.

The Audit Bureau of Circulations (ABC) wields considerable power within the media sector as it records and regulates the number of publications circulated within the South African market. Smaller media organisations complain they are unserviced or at best under-serviced by this system, thereby denying them access to the advertising community.

Conclusion 17: Partnership with the mainstream media
In the authors' opinion, the MDDA could facilitate an ethical and mutually beneficial partnership between the mainstream media and the small media to encourage skills transfer through exchange, twinning and mentorship. This should be encouraged particularly on a local and provincial level.

Private and public broadcasters as well as the commercial mainstream print media should be considered an important set of partners for local media.

This partnership could explore a range of synergies between mainstream and small media, including:
- The migration of content from small to mainstream media at a local, provincial and national level. This could help, in part, with tackling some of the SABC's language diversity problems. One option could be the use of 'stringers' trained by and based in small media organisations. Another could be the idea of 'public access time slots' on the SABC already enshrined in a 'Declaration of Intent' signed by the SABC in 1996.
- Skills transfer from mainstream to small media (and vice versa). This could include joint training, twinning, mentorship and staff exchanges.
- A structured internship or job placement opportunities from small to mainstream media community for volunteer interns (as opposed to core staff).

Such arrangements need to be sensitive to the independence, ownership and control of small media. Mechanisms must be found to avoid the poaching of key staff from small to commercial media. The PDU's suggestion of a Code of Practice to govern such relationships is a good one and should be facilitated by the MDDA in co-operation with networks such as the NAB, IMA, NCRF and PMSA.

4.5 Financial modelling

The community and independent media sector has a total annual expenditure of around R115 million. This can be broken down into the following components:
- Radio   R34.5 million
- Print   R34.4 million
- Multimedia and audiovisual media   R6.2 million
- Service providers   R40.0 million

The following provides some indication of the income of local radio, print, multimedia and service providers, taken from the database:
- Print   65 per cent of print organisations derive income from advertising
             11 per cent of print organisations derive income from donors
- Multimedia 8 per cent of multimedia organisations derive income from advertising
             8 per cent of multimedia organisations derive income from donors
- Radio   85 per cent of radio stations derive income from advertising
             43 per cent of radio stations derive income from donors

4.5.1 Analysing the environment

Looking at the funding environment, it is a miracle that the print sector has survived at all. Small print has generally not been able to access what funding there has been for small media, as the bulk of this has gone to radio. Neither has it benefited from the funding directed at audiovisual media as it seems to fall outside the official definition of arts and culture. The sector has only survived through its ability to tap into other income generating opportunities.

Analysis and conclusions

Audiovisual media has been more fortunate in that it falls under the ambit of 'cultural industries' and is thus benefiting from funding from the MAPPP SETA, the National Lottery, the NFVF, the NAC and other arts and culture funding opportunities. The MDDA should recognise that it is not carrying audiovisual media on its own. A niche does need to be found, however, for the MDDA's funding interventions and opportunities for co-funding of audiovisual needs to be explored. Until such time as community video has access to airtime it will not be able to generate an income for its products. The opportunity of a 'window' or 'public access time slot' on SABC or another broadcaster should unlock this potential.

Multimedia initiatives have generally benefited from technical support from the USF, among other government interventions. Many multimedia initiatives are struggling for survival because these interventions have not been conducive to long-term sustainability. These centres are usually aimed at providing access to information technology and services (including media). Multimedia centres have great potential to tap into income from local business for administrative and business services (such as design and DTP), computer training and a host of highly fundable services. But many lack the expertise to take advantage of these opportunities. Some multimedia projects operate in the context of MPCCs thus benefiting from 'in-kind' support in the form of a shared building and other infrastructure. This, and huge levels of volunteer effort, have ensured their continued survival.

Community radio stations have made some progress in attracting advertising. However, a recent report indicates that while the estimated listenership of community radio had increased from 8.8 per cent of total listenership in March 1999 to 10.8 per cent by December 2000, adspend had fallen from R8.3 million (for community radio) in 1999 to R7 million in 2000 (Tleane 2001: 18). This area clearly needs urgent attention.

The comparative total adspend for the radio sector amounted to R922 million in 1999 and R1.2 billion in 2000. An evaluation of community radio conducted between 1997 and 2001 estimates community radio has an estimated 1.6 million listeners across South Africa (Dooms 2001: 1).

However, significant gains have been made towards generating programming sponsorships with many local and international NGOs, foundations, and government departments. This is likely to be a central focus of foreign donor funding in the future. The sale of airtime (MTN, cell C and Vodacom) appears to be a common and important source of income for the sector.

Fourteen service providers were prepared to supply detailed financial details. From this data, it can be seen that the overwhelming bulk of income for the sector comes from international donors, followed by 'self-generated' income and much smaller proportions from government, the corporate sector and from South African sources.

Service providers make up a large slice of the total value of the sector (R40 million out of a total of R115 million). There is a surprisingly high degree of self-generated funding by the service providers, which indicates they are beginning to diversify their services and generate their own income. This needs to be encouraged and facilitated.

The people's voice

It is evident from the responses that international donor funding is decreasing, and quickly. This should ring warning bells in a sector that is already overly dependent on this source of funding. Some service providers report that they are dependent on international donors to the tune of between 75 per cent and 96 per cent.

Among major international donors who have announced plans to implement significant reductions in their contributions to the South African local media sector are the Open Society Foundation and the Ford Foundation. The Dutch funder, Netherlands Institute vir Zuidelike Afrika (NIZA) is probably the only exception. NIZA has been funding radio, film, print and internet projects in the region for the last five years, and plans to continue this support in the foreseeable future. It provides technical assistance, training, institutional development (but not equipment) and has a 2.3 million Euro budget (R16 million) for the region, which is due to increase. Other funders though, such as the Communication Assistance Foundation (CAF), have signalled their interest in sponsoring regional programmes rather than only South African ones.

There is a common reluctance among funders to provide capital for equipment and especially for consumables, rental, overheads and salaries. The main sources of international funding in the sector include the Open Society Foundation, Ford Foundation, Kaizer Foundation, Kellogg, Unicef, SAIH, NIZA, NORAD, OSISA, WACC, DFID, FES, Unesco, DANCED, the Embassy of Finland, the British Council and the Heinrich Bohl Foundation.

Funding from South African, non-governmental sources, is either stable or gradually increasing. Principal sources include the NLF, the Nelson Mandela Children's Fund and the CGE.

There is extremely limited funding coming from government sources at this time with only small amounts emanating from the various SETAs engaged in the sector. Only Create-SA, the arts and culture component of the MAPPP SETA appears to be providing limited funds (to audiovisual media) at this point. While there is funding for the arts, only film and video are deemed to be part of arts and culture. The DoC is only giving equipment to community radio.

The NFVF is only channelling funds to audiovisual projects, mainly to the independent production sector. The USF (via USA) is only funding telecentres, while local councils are focused mainly on arts and culture or radio. The identification of potential sources of funding, and especially the leveraging of government funds, could well be an important role of the MDDA.

On the other hand, corporate social investment appears to be very low in the sector, suggesting small media organisations and service providers are simply not tapping in to the private sector. The MDDA must ensure that training and other interventions builds the capacity of small media to leverage funding from the private sector through sponsorship deals and through promoting the attractions of the small media to the private sector itself. Some sort of incentive (tax relief) to stimulate investment in the sector might be considered and proposed to the finance ministry. The case study research demonstrates a palpable lack of support from local business, and in particular from 'white' business.

ANALYSIS AND CONCLUSIONS

A fundamental problem here is the focus of advertisers on affluent audiences. This is a section of the population for which the small media sector does not provide a service. Only one of the case studies reported success in advertising sales. Underlying this is an uncertainty over how to approach the local business sector together with an absence of marketing and advertising skills. Both of these were ranked at the very top of the skills needs articulated in the survey by the participants. It is clear that some sort of intervention from the MDDA would be useful here (see conclusions). An encouraging memorandum of understanding between the MDDA and SACOB, for example, might assist small media in getting a foot in the door of local companies. There is obviously an important training dimension to accessing the private sector.

It is similarly the case that the sector battles to access funders and does not know who to approach or how to approach them. Skills are lacking in planning, budgeting, proposal writing and reporting. Many of the case studies identified this as a problem. The completion of adequate business plans in the sector was infrequent and even fewer accompanied the business plans with technology plans.

While Section 21 companies are a frequent vehicle for community media organisations, Hagg has pointed out that this does not allow for receiving government funding except for grants for specific projects (Hagg 2002: 5).

The case study data suggests that seriously weak financial management systems are in place in the sector (together with numeracy problems). In general these systems comprise receipts and cheque requisitions. This severely limits the capacity of the organisations to attain sustainability.

4.5.2 Strategies for unlocking financial resources

The issue of financial sustainability cannot be looked at in isolation from HRD, institutional development, networking and partnerships as spelt out in the above sections. In addition to these, below are a number of suggested strategies aimed at unlocking financial resources for small media.

South African broadcasting regulations allow for commercial income for community broadcasters through advertising. This is not materialising for a range of reasons, many of which have been mentioned throughout this report. The capacity for income generation through advertising clearly needs to be supported. However, advertising is not the only answer. Arguably, the same reason that is used to justify a subsidy for the public broadcaster (providing a public service) can be applied to community media. The latter has similar, if not more stringent, public service obligations.

A US based community television producer, Jesikah Maria Ross, points out that there are very few, if any, cases where commercial considerations have not impacted negatively on community television's production and programming commitments to disadvantaged, minority or counter-cultural groups (Aldridge 1997).

As a starting premise, the authors agree with the sentiment that community media may never be totally self-sustainable – at least on a cost recovery basis based on market-related activities. Funding small media and, in particular, community media is a creative, dynamic and complex process involving various sources of income and funding linked to services offered. Small media is operating in an environment that is changing as fast as the pace of technological innovation. Its survival will depend on its ability to mutate, adapt and innovate.

Arguably, community media should strive towards a mixed economy where no one source of income dominates or creates dependency.

This is because:
- An over dependence on government threatens editorial independence.
- Over-emphasis on funders is unrealistic and results in 'mission drag', i.e. designing interventions around funding trends.
- An over dependence on commercial revenues would threaten the social and developmental orientation of community media.
- A diversity of income sources makes sound business sense.

The following international examples are useful as the high costs involved in community television have forced practitioners to come up with sophisticated and innovative funding models:

The Australian experience
Financing Australian CTV is based on the principle of 'a third, a third, a third' – one-third government support (spread over local council and arts and culture) as the bottom-line 'anchor' source of funding, one-third market based activities (programme sales, equipment hire, services), and one-third funds raised through fund-raising events.

According to Michael Thompson, of the Community Broadcasting Association of Australia: 'The Australian experience highlights the need for bottom line, base funding from the government. But the government wants something back for its contribution. In Perth the government offers 100 000 dollars per annum in exchange for a third of air time on educational programming' (Thorne 1998: 238).

The Danish experience
In 1998, Denmark had numerous types of audiovisual funding models including local access television, film and video workshops, video access centres and film schools. These were funded by a variety of government departments including local municipalities, the Film Institute and donors. While most of this has been dismantled in the wake of a new, conservative government, the models remain useful.

According to Lars Bo Kimergaard, of the Danish VideOlympiad: 'The problem for community TV stations is that there is no bottom line, sustaining source of funding.' In Denmark there is a strong relationship between local access television, film workshops and the Danish national broadcaster. This secures some income from licence fees (Thorne 1998: 239).

International donors supporting the development of community media in the southern African region share information through a Funders' Forum. According to some funders who responded to the survey there still remain some overlaps. Donors who are invested in the sector, such as NIZA and the OSF, have expressed their interest in closer liaison with the MDDA and other government funders.

Analysis and conclusions

With NIZA's focus on 'capacity enhancement' for community media and commercial press, it is likely to be a significant partner for the MDDA. The OSF has been the biggest single contributor to community media over the past ten years and has injected about R8 million a year into the sector. OSF is currently scaling down their support in preparation for their withdrawal in 2005. This is likely to have a significant impact on the sector.

Conclusion 18: Unlocking and synergising funding interventions
A critical role for the MDDA will be to unlock and co-ordinate funding efforts across the board, in particular with regard to government-related agencies. Improved communication and information sharing will help funders to hone in on their focus areas, avoid duplication and plug gaps. For those areas where government funding remains largely untapped, the MDDA could help to unlock funds expeditiously. Table 2 suggests how government funding might be synergised.

Table 2: Suggested framework for funding organisations

Organisation	What they could fund
DoC	Equipment Programming (move to Broadcast Production Fund)
NFVF	Co-funding of video (or multimedia) access centres
USF/USA	Access to ICT in the context of community multimedia centres
Local council	Infrastructure support (e.g. building) and services rendered
MAPPP SETA	Skills programmes and learnerships
Lottery	Video access centres (as part of cultural sector plan currently being developed)
Broadcast Production Fund	MDDA should probe the status of this initiative, which could be absorbed by the NFVF (for video) and the MDDA (for radio). If it is not on the cards, the MDDA should explore cross-subsidisation from private broadcasters to community broadcasters via the MDDA and/or the NFVF. Either way the MDDA should work in partnership with such a body.
Social services	Work-based training programmes (volunteers) for unemployed youth (by community media organisations)
Arts councils	Video projects
Film Offices	Video access centres
DTI	Start up loan finance

What is interesting about the above is that there is plenty of potential support for video, implying that, although video is more expensive than radio, there is more opportunity for co-funding in this area.

The MDDA would do well to learn from the lessons learned by other donors such as the IMDT, the OSF and NIZA to guide its own work. These lessons, drawn from interviews as well as from service provider responses, include:

THE PEOPLE'S VOICE

- Work in a developmental way and maintain a high degree of two-way interaction between donor and grantees.
- Avoid duplication and fragmentation through networking with different stakeholders.
- Understand the laws and regulations governing the sector and influencing policy-making.
- Don't focus on one medium.
- Implement monitoring and evaluation from the start to the end of the project.
- Avoid 'hit and run' funding (or once-off) funding without follow-ups.
- Impress on local media the importance of diversifying their donor base.
- Use participatory methods in designing strategies and methodologies.
- 'Communicate, communicate, communicate'.
- Tight financial controls, particularly for new, emerging projects, which might require monthly financial acquittals.

Conclusion 19: MDDA funding priorities
The following are suggested funding priorities in light of the research undertaken by this project to date.

The IMA has suggested a number of recommendations concerning the role of the MDDA when it comes to funding. For the purposes of giving the MDDA a broad range of opinion, these are as follows:
- The MDDA should balance funding across all media not just radio.
- The MDDA should limit cash handouts or grants, except in emergencies.
- The MDDA should not be handing grants to individual media projects, but to initiatives of use to the whole sector, such as a national advertising clearing house, joint service bureau for copy editing and lay-out, legal advice and administrative support.
- The MDDA should create entities that will make a profit in the long-term, such as independent commercial printers that will hand on discounted services to other sector players.
- The MDDA should not duplicate training and should focus, instead, on producing resource materials or subsidising current trainers to produce training materials.

Conclusion 20: Partnerships and resource-sharing
In the opinion of the authors, the MDDA should encourage partnerships and resources sharing, as suggested through the CMS or MCCC model. This model promotes financial sustainability in that it encourages resource sharing with like-minded local structures thus reducing costs. In addition, it aims to diversify the services offered by local media and therefore the income generating opportunities.

According to the GCIS, community communication centres should contain a combination of facilities and services including, amongst other things, a) administrative, b) training, c) community media/cultural development services, and d) SMME support services. Some of the services that could be offered by CMS, are shown in Table 3.

Analysis and conclusions

Table 3: Suggested functions for community communications centres

Service	Cost recovery
Educational content: health, gender, environment, local government elections, etc.	NGOs/donors Corporate social investment Government
Training and development services: Educational support programmes for schools, tertiary education, vocational training, e-learning	Department of Education Social services Seta
Job centre: job listings, job and internship placements, info on training opportunities, support with CV writing and job applications	Government
Government information Assistance with grant applications	GCIS Local government Provincial government Various ministries
Commercial media production: design and DTP services video production, etc.	Government Business
Stringer operation and content output deals *Syndication*	Private/public media
Business/administrative services: phones, typing, fax photocopying, e-mail, Internet	Local business
Communication services: social marketing, communications training	Government NGOs
Advertising sales (local, provincial and national)	Local business National procurement
Equipment hire	Local SMMEs, government
Airtime sale (perhaps linked to commercial programming slots)	Corporate sponsors, churches, NGOs
Community advise/information services, e.g. SMME support	DTI
Other services: tourism, coffee shop, craft centre	Tourists, locals

(Source: GCIS MCCC draft document 2003, CMS Task Team Report, 2003)

Conclusion 21: Human resource development

The success of the above two strategies rests on the ability of small media to operate at a fairly sophisticated level, particularly with regards to managing a complex web of partnerships. While this is a major risk factor, capacity for project management can and must be built into training interventions as a matter of priority.

Other training interventions, that directly impact on financial sustainability, that have already been mentioned, include:
- Developing a business plan;
- Planning, budgeting, fund-raising, evaluation and report writing skills;
- Financial administration and management; and
- Marketing and advertising skills.

Conclusion 22: Other sustainability strategies

The authors would like to propose a number of suggestions to facilitate sustainability in the sector. These are:
- The MDDA, in consultation with the networks, should commission research into the feasibility of, and to develop a model for, a national advertising procurement agency to unlock national and provincial adspend and programming sponsorship deals for local media. The structure should take into account both national and provincial procurement and link with provincial hubs or other local networks. The agency could be based on a franchise model with small provincial agencies depending on expertise and support from a national body. Research should also look into the ownership structure of this agency, which should, at the very least, be part owned by 'the sector' (national networks?). This agency has been proposed by the IMA, the NCRF and the PDU and is a high priority.
- The above should be done in conjunction with a new system for circulation verification (PDU) and the calculation of amps figures (NCRF).
- The PDU has called for a new arrangement for printing procurement, for collective printing in return for good rates and credit options.
- Small media organisations that provide public access to ICTs should receive a discounted tariff for connectivity, such as the e-rate for schools. The logical source of funding for an e-rate would be the USF administered by the Universal Service Agency (USA). This could also be extended to a 'community tariff' that applies to the cellular operators Community Service Telephones (CMS TT Report, 2003).
- The creation of an environment in which small media can band together by assisting with setting up of syndicates.
- In the hey-day of broadcast liberalisation in the mid-1990s the NCMF gave serious consideration to the establishment of an investment vehicle similar to the Mineworkers Investment Corporation to pursue investment opportunities in the burgeoning private broadcast arena (Thorne 1996). Investments were to be made in related spheres in order to 'add value' to the investment through the direct involvement of beneficiaries. Due to a lack of capacity, this idea never came to fruition, but it remains an opportunity, particularly for community television, with the next round of private, regional broadcast licensing around the corner.

4.6 Networking and information

As has come up repeatedly in this report, effective networking, information sharing and co-ordination are vital for the success of small media. This needs to take place at all levels, both horizontally and vertically, at the local, provincial, national and international levels. The following networks are relevant to local media:
- Sectoral networks:
  - Community radio: NCRF
  - Independent print: IMA
  - Video access centres: part of broader industry networks, such as the National TV and Video Association (NTVA)
  - Community print: none
- Related networks:
  - MPCC network (via GCIS)
  - Telecentre network (via USA)
  - National Federation of Community Arts Centres

ANALYSIS AND CONCLUSIONS

- Industry networks (includes community, public and private media):
  - MISA: SADC network concerned with policy, advocacy and media development, includes a South African chapter
  - NAB: National Association of Broadcasters

The research from this project suggests that the sector is well-networked – though frequently this is ad hoc in nature – and there is evidence that a lot of collaboration in different forms is taking place. There is also a tremendous amount of duplication, most especially in the urban centres. There is competition too, and not always of the healthy sort. This means service providers end up chasing funds and offering the same services (mission drag). It is clear that, at best, training and service provision is uncoordinated and the sector as a whole is not moving forward on the basis of an integrated, national strategy. Community radio stations included in the survey reported weak communications with the NCRF.

It was a general concern amongst those participating in this project that the MDDA should seek to tap into the expertise that has been developed in the sector over years of practice, by service providers, rather than reinventing the wheel and causing further duplication of services rendered. Indeed, one of the primary goals of this project is to audit service provision in the sector so as to avoid this potential pitfall.

The survey conducted in this research report asked service providers to indicate how they obtained information about the sector, what sort of information they would like and how they would like to receive the information. The questions were posed with a view to assisting the MDDA to clarify its own possible role with regard to facilitating the effective gathering and use of information among service providers. Conclusions emanating from this process follow below.

Conclusion 23: Information dissemination

During the course of the research conducted for this study, a need was expressed for information on all the different forms of media (radio, television, film and video, etc.) in one place, updates on what the other service providers are doing and information on what government is doing (in particular, initiatives emanating from the DoC and from the MDDA).

A common wish expressed was for a regularly updated electronic news and information service. Other information needs include:
- Skills development for staff training;
- Public health information;
- A website to cater for special interest groups, e.g. HIV/AIDS, gender, youth, etc., including training materials, links for interaction and exchange and links to other relevant sites;
- Policy and regulatory developments;
- Best practice models;
- A database of potential staff, freelance trainers and consultants;
- Post vacancies;
- Opportunities for broadcasters with regard to training and development;
- Updated information on new community organisations in the region and in South Africa;

The people's voice

- Information on issues such as human rights, gender, race, children's rights, etc.;
- Information on issues related to media diversity and development;
- Information on issues related to the development of civil society;
- Information on the media in general;
- New developments, trends and new ventures in the sector;
- Funding opportunities;
- Statistics and surveys;
- Government tenders;
- Opportunities for co-operation;
- 'Training the trainer' opportunities; and
- Management information, techniques, training tools, etc.

On the issue of how service providers would like to receive this information, most agreed that electronically would be the most appropriate mechanism. There appeared to be a need for a sector website (though there are service providers capable of being tasked to provide this), a community radio newsletter, an e-mail mailing list, conferences and workshops.

Conclusion 24: Who does what?
Service providers were asked to outline the roles they expected to be filled by the MDDA, the national networks, service providers and government. These, which do not necessarily reflect the views of the authors, were described as follows:

4.6.1 Role of the MDDA

According to the service providers surveyed in this research, the MDDA was expected to undertake the following tasks:
- Funding and grant making to small, (independent and community) media;
- Funding to service providers and networks to assist in the creation of an enabling environment and to bolster co-ordination and collaboration;
- Research;
- Leveraging resources from other government departments (such as communications contracts) as well as from the private sector and/or international donors and co-ordinate interventions to prevent duplication;
- Policy development and alignment;
- Assist/train small media sector to write funding applications, in collaboration with service providers;
- Lobbying for a higher sector profile and to stimulate debate on the role of the community media sector;
- Assist with publication of manuals and textbooks; and
- Advise sector on issues like setting up an advertising department, distribution and debt collection. Material already available from (e.g. United States) should be adapted and localised.

4.6.2 Role of the national networks

These networks include organisations such as the IMA, NAB, NCRF and MISA. According to the survey, service providers considered the following to be the role of these networks:
- Networking and information dissemination;
- Mobilisation and awareness raising;
- Encouraging co-ordination and collaboration;
- Setting standards;

Analysis and conclusions

- Providing a forum for interaction and debate;
- Policy development and advocacy;
- Providing the communication interface between the MDDA and the sector;
- Facilitating resource sharing, e.g. training manuals and materials, equipment, research data; and
- Research.

4.6.3 Role of service providers

The service providers defined their own role within the sector, as follows:
- Provide services to develop the small media sector that promote sustainable growth and development. This was seen as a function that the MDDA and the networks should specifically not take on;
- Enhance quality of content;
- Make information known about services they provide to all;
- Co-develop and support a national strategy;
- Assist/train media organisations to write funding applications, in collaboration with MDDA;
- Implementation partners;
- Provision of expertise; and
- Monitoring.

4.6.4 Role of government departments

A greater level of interaction and consultation with the sector was urged by service providers in the survey. Service providers outlined the role of various government departments as follows:

MAPPP SETA should:
- Provide funding for training.

The NFVF should:
- Co-fund community video access centres; and
- Support VRCs in CMSs.

GCIS should:
- Leverage government communication budgets for social marketing campaigns run by community media networks; and
- Develop simple guides, like the pocket Constitution, to assist government access to the media, and vice versa.

The DoC should:
- Develop a technical maintenance plan for rural areas;
- Develop partnerships with media NGOs which have the capacity to work in content development;
- Provide funding for technical roll-out but not necessarily implement; and
- Provide policy framework and enable legislation.

The people's voice

The USF should, through the universal service fund:
- Provide universal access to ICTs in the context of telecentres, MPCCs and CMSs;
- Co-operate with DoC to develop a technical maintenance plan for rural areas; and
- Subsidise a discounted tariff for connectivity for community multimedia services: E-rate.

Conclusion 25: Strengthening the networks

The authors of this report believe the independent and community media networks need to be strengthened and supported. There is also a compelling argument for the NCRF to expand its membership to include community video, multimedia and possibly community print.

There is also a need for improved communication and co-ordination between the community and independent media networks as well as with the 'related' and 'industry' networks.

4.7 Content development

The issue of content has been referred to in passing while discussing the mainstream media and government's role in the sector. Figure 5 indicates where most organisations access their content.

Figure 5: Where content is sourced

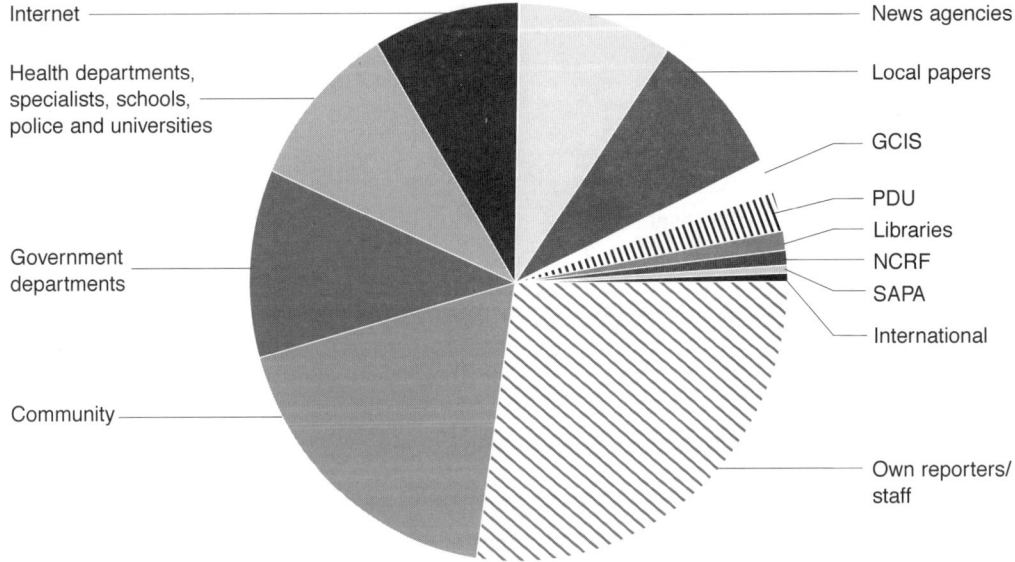

Analysis and conclusions

As can be seen, content is largely self-generated or taken from government with less reliance on service providers or agencies. International research suggests a key obstacle to community media accessing relevant content is a lack of awareness of what is already available.

The whole issue of the external provision of content for community radio, no matter how developmental or educational, has generated much tension in the sector. On the one hand community radio stations stand accused of being 'inaccessible' by/to NGOs. On the other hand, community radio stations resent being regarded as a 'megaphone' for other peoples' messages. Community radio stations, often struggling for their own survival, feel they have a right to charge for this service. The NCRF has argued that this trend towards externally produced programming does not build the capacity of community radio stations to produce developmentally oriented programming themselves.

The way in which this has been dealt with has been to charge outside users for this service, as in the case of the GCIS, which uses community radio to disseminate government information. Alternatively, NGOs are expected to provide training to community broadcasters if they wish to introduce programming dealing with social justice issues, such as is the case with Idasa and Workers World Radio. While this may be a costly and time-consuming exercise, it does serve to build sustainable capacity in radio stations to carry this content.

It would seem as if programming sponsorship is a growing funding opportunity. Add to this the untapped corporate sponsorship and this could potentially be a very lucrative activity. NGOs, with the fund-raising skills and national focus, could play a major role in unlocking this potential.

There does however remain an important role for local NGOs, CBOs and other user groups in the production of content. Community radio stations should consider themselves a kind of decentralised communications web (Scott 1996). They should encourage local groups to participate in content generation (by, for instance, training local NGOs in handheld microphone and recorder usage). On the whole, community media organisations seem constantly to overlook the importance of enabling people from their communities to pop in to their offices and exercise their right to communicate. There is thus an over emphasis on quality programming when, for example, an on-air interview with someone from the community also provides relevant material with local appeal.

Community media organisations are frequently not providing a forum for debate in which prevailing attitudes and opinions are challenged and a diversity of voices is allowed to be heard. Community participation should not be limited to participation in AGMs and talk shows.

Icasa has identified four key problems faced by community radio organisations in South Africa with regard to content:
- Record companies prefer to deal with bigger stations.
- Distribution of music is difficult, especially if radio stations are far from Johannesburg.
- Not enough reissues are released by record companies.
- Record companies don't release enough music for community media's target audiences.

A review of the data indicates that while print organisations communicated through their products in a total of eight languages and multi-media organisations used five languages, community radio was the outlet for 15 languages. Small media/community multimedia has the potential to play a critically important role in developing local language content on the world wide web.

Some final remarks on content, which have all been incorporated into other conclusions:
- Content is a training issue (in the production of 'quality' content) but it is also a media education issue in that stations and publishers need to be aware of the role of small media as a tool for citizen communication, local dialogue and social change. This ties to the need to strengthen links with NGOs and civic structures.
- Small media need training in participatory audience/market research.
- Community media needs to tap into local culture, music, theatre and sports events. This once again points to the need to build partnerships between CACs/practitioners and local media.
- The small media sector needs to be encouraged and trained to tap into programming sponsorship from the private sector, in addition to government and donors. This could be linked to a national (social) marketing procurement agency.

Conclusion 26: National local media news agency
On several occasions, recommendations have been forthcoming from other stakeholders with regard to the creation of regional news agencies alongside an effective, independent, national news agency for the small media sector (MDT Report 2000 IMA). There appears to be considerable merit in the suggestion although there may be existing initiatives that could be supported in this regard. The authors conclude that the notion of a national news agency to service the small media should be investigated.

4.8 Technical sustainability

South Africa is positioning itself globally in relation to the development of an information society. Much has been said regarding the impact of digitisation and convergence on the media sector and the need for small media to hitch a ride on the information super-highway. All indications are that this is already happening, organically. Benjamin's research on telecentres has shown that successful telecentres are ones that have managed to focus on content and have established ties with small media structures (2001). Telecentres on their own are not viable. The ones that are doing well are those that are providing information services and training (Benjamin 2001).

Convergence is likely to have far-reaching impact on small media. The National Convergence Policy Colloquium agreed that, 'universal access and service should be more than just access to basic telephony; it should include access to advanced services such as broadband, infrastructure, broadcasting, multimedia and postal services' (Thorne 1996: 94). Convergence and the policies that enable it, present both opportunities and challenges to local media and it is imperative that small media networks keep ahead of and input into the policy process. This work seems to consume an enormous amount of the NCRF resources.

This research, although not designed to explore technical issues in any great detail, has generated several observations with relevance to the notion of technical sustainability.

Analysis and conclusions

These include:
- Almost all of the print media organisations had access to e-mail (80 out of 83) and most radio stations (72 out of 81). Community radio stations are using the Internet to promote research, programme sharing and information dissemination.
- Multimedia centres are starting to emerge in remote rural areas, often in the context of an MPCC or telecentre.
- Networks are using e-mail and Internet as effective networking and programme sharing tools.

Some problems have been ascertained. These include:
- Many stations are struggling with inappropriate or incorrectly installed studio and transmission equipment.
- Staff of both radio stations and telecentres receive little training in operating and maintaining equipment.
- Many stations are located in rural areas where there is no support and as a result equipment often remains unutilised due to minor technical problems.
- Due to the prohibitive costs of software, there appears to be frequent usage of illegal software in the sector. In a survey of software needs conducted within the case study enquiry, the four most desired packages were: Cool Edit 2000, e-mail and Internet access, Pastel Accounting (1-6) and Explorer. A variety of other software was listed.
- The cost of connectivity is too high for many small media groups.
- Besides the obvious fact that many local media do not have sufficient technical resources, many small media organisations lack the human resource capacity to operate and maintain basic equipment. For those based in rural areas this is made worse by a lack of technical support in the area.

Conclusion 27: Sector technology plan
In the opinion of the authors, the MDDA needs to conduct research in order to develop a technology plan for the small media sector. This research should explore appropriate adaptable, compatible, affordable, user-friendly hardware and software to inform purchase choices for the small media sector.

Research should explore the potential of open source software with a view to providing it to the sector through a website. Such research may inform the bulk equipment purchase deals – perhaps involving contributions from relevant embassies.

Conclusion 28: Radio station maintenance plan
A maintenance plan for community radio stations clearly needs to be developed. The MDDA, NCRF and the DoC should work together to develop a maintenance plan for community radio, particularly those based in rural areas. This could be extended to include all forms of small media. The plan could take the form of a franchise of black-owned SMMEs operating in the provinces with national support. The South African NGO Network (Sangonet) and Globecom could be drawn in to assist if not already involved.

4.9 Further research

This project also set out to include some suggestions on future research that the MDDA should think of commissioning to aid its work.

The people's voice

These suggestions include:
- Research on the feasibility and modelling of a national procurement agency (see 'Financial modelling' section);
- Research on a technology plan for the community media sector including into open source software (see 'ICTs');
- Research on the need for a management services agency, suggested by PDU and IMA, including the structure, function and activities of such an agency;
- A user-friendly handbook and website;
- Rewrite and update the policy section in this report in basic, accessible language and in other South African languages to stimulate debate among small media practitioners;
- Follow-up research looking at penetration of public and private media and cross-referencing with own exercise and development of a grading system with least to most serviced areas in country;
- Research on region-wide local media initiatives and the creation or support of a regional small media network.

5 Conclusion

South Africa's small media sector has enormous potential on a wide range of fronts. It can provide skills, access to information, education, empowerment, accountability and development, to name but a few. Its capacity to do these, and many other things, is widely recognised. There is a voluminous list of research from many continents that supports what has largely become a matter of global consensus. What remains is not, therefore, to justify the importance of small media or to debate its merits, but to understand it within our own context and to plan how best to facilitate its growth and development.

The work done in South Africa so far on the various components of small media has been uneven, with a special focus given to community radio in the post-apartheid period since 1994. In spite of the fact that many connected to small media believe in similar outcomes, in practice, the management and development of the sector has been disjointed and poorly co-ordinated. The consequence has been a gradual but insufficient improvement in media diversity, a situation the MDDA has been charged to address.

The extent of this diversity is captured by the data and analysis presented in this report, which is the first to consider all the component parts of the small media sector in the current era. The conclusions, which cover a broad range of areas from sustainability and distribution to further research, will hopefully equip the MDDA to begin its work quickly and efficiently.

There are naturally debates within the sector and affecting it that have been contested for years by different groups. This has been exacerbated by the political transition that has formed a fragmented and even heated context for these debates. The authors of this report have tried to present all the key research on the small media sector that has emerged over the last few years and combine it in one document. Reports, evaluations, conference proceedings, task group investigations, journal articles and institutional knowledge have all been tapped in the bid to present to the MDDA as thorough and comprehensive a picture as possible. Where there have been disagreements, we have reflected these. But there are also many areas in which people who care about small media agree. We have sought to present these once more with the appropriate acknowledgement of their original source.

We must emphasise, once more, that this report does not represent the official view or strategic intention of the MDDA. It is merely a collaborative research project aimed at garnering as much information as possible about the small media sector.

A central concern has been to explore the notion of sustainability in the sector: what it means, how it works and what can be done to facilitate it. Sustainability, as we have argued, is a complex process. But it is not an unfathomable one. Very substantial progress can be made with the correct models and strategies in place. This report presents a holistic view of sustainability which combines the economic with the social aspects, as well as a number of ways in which it can be encouraged to flourish.

Another vital aspect of this project and of our findings is the impact of convergence on the development of the small media sector. The economic spin-offs, social benefits and strategic implications of convergence have forced an elemental rethink of the role and future of the small media sector. There is no question that synergising small media efforts with the objectives and infrastructure of other Information Society initiatives will give disproportionately greater impetus to the sector as a whole. It will also greatly assist the level of participation enjoyed by communities and the capacity of small media to fulfil constitutional imperatives, including freedom of expression, cultural and linguistic diversity, and access to information.

Another important aspect of this report has been the dovetailing of the interests of the small commercial media sector with those of community media organisations. Both have their origins in very different schools of thought. The recommended approach in this report is one that embraces a mixed economy outlook that the authors believe takes the best of both worlds. This is certainly not the time to be excluding components of the sector on the grounds of motive rather than delivery. If there is one overriding conclusion, it is the need for greater co-ordination and communication. This must be a key function of the MDDA, however it defines its operational strategy. There is patently too much overlap, duplication and wastage among small media organisations, service providers and within government. There is also a great deal of ignorance surrounding the role of the sector, the MDDA and, again, of government. Bringing clarity to these issues through the compilation of firm guidelines and crisp policy is another important goal.

During the course of this project, a great deal of information and data has been gathered. Some of it has been available but has been located with different institutions, some of it has been published internationally but has not been presented locally and some has been collected in person-to-person interviews. The overall picture is of a sector that is struggling but which has enormous potential. With the right amount of assistance in the right areas, the small media sector will prove to be an invaluable dimension to the national project of improving people's lives and entrenching a truly democratic way of life.

APPENDIX

Questionnaires

The following questionnaires were used to gather information and data about organisations within the sector. The capacity enhancement needs assessment questionnaire was conducted face-to-face in the field by media researchers while the service provider questionnaire was either faxed or e-mailed to us on completion.

Capacity enhancement needs assessment questionnaire

I ORGANISATIONAL DETAILS

Organisation: _____
Name: _____
Position: _____
Postal address: _____
Telephone: _____
Fax: _____
Cell phone: _____
E-mail: _____
Website: _____

1. **In what year was your organisation founded?** _____

2. **What is the legal status of your organisation?**
   - Section 21 company ☐
   - Trust ☐
   - Close Corporation ☐
   - Other: ☐

3. **What is the goal/social objective of your organisation?** _____

4. **What services do you offer?**
   - Media training ☐
   - Media production ☐
   - Advocacy ☐
   - Broadcasting/distribution ☐
   - Providing access to facilities ☐
   - Job creation ☐
   - Other: ☐

5. **What kind of media do you use?**
   - Radio ☐
   - Audiovisual ☐
   - Print ☐
   - ICTs ☐
   - Visual arts ☐
   - Performing arts ☐
   - Posters ☐

The people's voice

    Banners ☐
    T-shirts ☐
    Web content ☐
    On-line publishing/distribution ☐
    Other: ☐

6. **Why have you chosen to focus on this particular form of media?** _____
_____

7. **What synergies, opportunities and challenges are associated with these media?**
_____

8. **How would you describe your organisation?**
    Community media ☐
    Independent media ☐
    A service organisation ☐
    Collective ☐
    Other: ☐

9. **Depending on how you answered the question above, how do you see the role of your organisation in development, democracy and other social objectives?**
_____
_____
_____
_____

10. **Who is the target of your organisation?**
    Youth ☐
    Women ☐
    Farm workers ☐
    Unemployed ☐
    Unions ☐
    Schools ☐
    General population ☐
    Churches ☐
    Disabled ☐
    Civic structures ☐
    NGOs ☐
    Other: ☐

11. **What is your geographical reach?**
_____
_____
_____
_____

Appendix

II INSTITUTIONAL MATTERS

12. How is your board constituted?

Name	Capacity	Representation/expertise

13. Who selects your organisation's board members?

- Current board members ☐
- Staff ☐
- The members of your organisation ☐
- Other: ☐

14. For what period do your board members hold tenureship? _____

15. How many board meetings did your organisation hold in 2001/2?
_____

16. Are minutes taken?
    Yes ☐   No ☐

17. Staff details:

Job title	Remuneration

As of today, what is the number of paid employees in your organisation?
Full time _____ Part time _____
Women _____ Men _____
Historically disadvantaged staff _____

THE PEOPLE'S VOICE

18. Does your organisation work with volunteers?
Yes ☐   No ☐
If yes, how many? _____
Please describe in what way your organisation is working with volunteers:
_____
_____

19. What capacity does your staff have?
This question is aimed at providing a general idea of your organisation's human resources skills and competencies. Please indicate the level of capacity on a scale of 1 (weak) to 5 (strong).

	1	2	3	4	5
Competency	☐	☐	☐	☐	☐
General competency	☐	☐	☐	☐	☐
Administration	☐	☐	☐	☐	☐
Meeting facilitation	☐	☐	☐	☐	☐
Financial management	☐	☐	☐	☐	☐
Fundraising	☐	☐	☐	☐	☐
Marketing, promotion, publicity	☐	☐	☐	☐	☐
Planning	☐	☐	☐	☐	☐
Human resource management	☐	☐	☐	☐	☐
Human resource practice	☐	☐	☐	☐	☐
Conflict management	☐	☐	☐	☐	☐
Negotiation	☐	☐	☐	☐	☐
Managing partnerships	☐	☐	☐	☐	☐
Project management	☐	☐	☐	☐	☐
Co-ordination of activities	☐	☐	☐	☐	☐
Community mobilisation	☐	☐	☐	☐	☐
Communication	☐	☐	☐	☐	☐
Media theory	☐	☐	☐	☐	☐
Media practice	☐	☐	☐	☐	☐
Skills training	☐	☐	☐	☐	☐
Computer literacy	☐	☐	☐	☐	☐

20. In which areas does the broader community access and participate in your organisation?
In governance ☐
In management ☐
In training programmes ☐
In content creation ☐
In supporting the project ☐
In an advisory capacity ☐
Through membership ☐
Other: ☐

21. How does the community participate in the above areas? _____
_____
_____

APPENDIX

III PARTNERSHIPS AND NETWORKING

22. Is your organisation a member of any network or does it derive support from any other service provider?

If so, please indicate your level of satisfaction with usefulness of the network/service provider on a scale of 1 (weak) to 5 (strong). Circle the appropriate number.

Name of network	Services provided	Effectiveness	Comments
		1 2 3 4 5	
		1 2 3 4 5	
		1 2 3 4 5	
		1 2 3 4 5	
		1 2 3 4 5	
		1 2 3 4 5	

23. Please list other partnerships and state the nature of those partnerships:

Name of partner	Nature of partnership

24. What other potential partners in your area could be of interest for future partnerships (e.g. telecentres, MPCCs, higher educational institutions, NGOs, civics, businesses, churches, local media, etc.)?

Potential partners	Synergy/opportunities	Comments/challenges

25. What other forms of media exist in the area?

- Daily newspaper ☐
- Weekly newspaper ☐
- Radio station ☐
- TV station ☐
- On-line media ☐
- Other: ☐

The people's voice

26. **How effective do you think they are in meeting the communication and information needs of all the people in the area?**
    Please indicate the level of effectiveness on a scale of 1 (not effective) to 5 (very effective).

1	2	3	4	5
☐	☐	☐	☐	☐

27. **Does your organisation have any formal links with media in the area?**
    Yes ☐   No ☐
    If yes, please specify: _____

28. **Does your organisation have a formal agreement with any government departments?**
    Yes ☐   No ☐
    If yes, please specify: _____

29. **Has your organisation been part of the Integrated Development Planning process?**
    Yes ☐   No ☐
    If yes, in what capacity? _____
    If no, why not? _____

30. **Is your organisation registered as a service provider with any government department?**
    Yes ☐   No ☐
    If yes, what service do you render? _____

IV SITUATION ANALYSIS

31. **Please describe the political environment in which you operate:**
    _____
    _____

32. **To what extent does the political environment impact on the work you do, positively or negatively?**
    _____
    _____

33. **To what extent has government involvement impacted on community ownership and control, content or editorial control?**
    _____
    _____

34. **What is the unemployment rate in your community?**
    Very high   ☐
    High   ☐
    Average   ☐
    Low   ☐
    Very low   ☐

APPENDIX

35. What social problems exist in the area in which you operate?

Unemployment ☐
Dependency on social grants ☐
Alcohol abuse ☐
Drug abuse ☐
Gangsterism ☐
Violence towards women and children ☐
Other: ☐

36. How are your programmes actively tackling these problems?

_____
_____

37. Please list the key industries providing work in your area:

_____
_____

38. What educational opportunities are there in your area?

Preschool ☐
Primary school ☐
High school ☐
University/Technikon ☐

39. Have you done any participatory research on the community's communication needs?

Yes ☐   No ☐
If yes, please specify: _____

40. Please list any key NGOs active in tackling development issues in the area:

_____
_____

41. Are you working together with any of these NGOs?

Yes ☐   No ☐
If no, why not? _____

V CONTENT

42. Please indicate the percentage of content in the following categories:

Category	Percentage
News and current affairs	
Documentary/actuality	
Talk shows	
Drama	
Music	

→

The people's voice

Category	Percentage
Religion	
Community affairs	
Sport	
Culture	
Features	
Profiles	
Information and announcements	
Other:	

43. Please indicate the percentage of content produced by the following contributors:

Contributor	Percentage
Staff	
Volunteers	
Partnership slots (e.g. NGOs)	
Airtime sales	
Other	

VI FINANCIAL AFFAIRS

44. What is your organisation's average annual budget?

_____
_____

45. What are your average monthly running costs?

_____
_____

46. Please describe your financial management systems:

_____
_____

47. Do you have a business plan?

Yes ☐   No ☐

APPENDIX

48. Please list your sources of income in the table below:

	Source of income	Percentage of overall budget	Comments
International donors			
South African donors			
Government funding			
Corporate social investment			
Self-generated income			

49. Does funding impact on content/editorial control?
   Yes ☐   No ☐
   If yes, how? _____

VII TRAINING

50. Please give details of previous training received:
Please indicate the level of effectiveness of the training on a scale of 1 (weak) to 5 (strong). Circle the appropriate number.

Service provider	Training offered	Date and duration	Effectiveness
			1 2 3 4 5
			1 2 3 4 5
			1 2 3 4 5
			1 2 3 4 5
			1 2 3 4 5

51. Please give details of your training needs in the following categories:

Priority	Training area	Training needed
	Education	
	Media literacy & gender awareness	☐
	Social communication/media in development	☐
	Human rights & democracy education	☐
	Political economy of the media	☐
	Media law & ethics	☐

→

Priority	Training area	Training needed
	Technical training	
	Writing skills	☐
	Journalism	☐
	Media planning	☐
	On-line publishing	☐
	DTP	☐
	Web design	☐
	Graphic design	☐
	Screen-printing	☐
	Video production	☐
	Photography	☐
	Newspaper/newsletter production	☐
	Radio production	☐
	Strategic use of ICTs for media production & distribution	☐
	Institutional capacity building	
	Advertising & sales	☐
	Marketing	☐
	Media management	☐
	Setting up a community radio/media project	☐
	Human resource management	☐
	Financial management	☐
	Business skills	☐
	Organisational development	☐
	Fundraising	☐
	Life skills	
	Conflict resolution	☐
	Starting up a small business	☐
	Personal development	☐
	Communication skills	☐
	Other	
		☐
		☐

Appendix

52. How would you like training to be delivered?
    Training on site ☐
    Training in your region together with people
        from other community media organisations ☐
    Ongoing on-site mentorship by fieldworker ☐

53. Who needs training?
    Volunteers ☐
    Staff ☐
    Board members ☐
    Other: ☐

54. What guarantees are there for people coming back from training, in terms of implementing and passing on their new skills?

_____
_____
_____
_____

55. What kind of support would your organisation be able to offer participants after a training course?
    Employment ☐
    Access to space ☐
    Access to equipment ☐
    Ensure further training ☐
    Monitoring and coaching ☐
    Other: ☐

56. Have you experienced any challenges associated with training and the development of your organisation?
    Yes ☐   No ☐
If yes, please specify the problems and suggest possible improvements/solutions:

_____
_____
_____
_____

57. What training, if any, does your organisation provide to users, volunteers or other community media centres?

_____
_____

VIII TECHNOLOGY

58. Please tick the relevant boxes below, list the quantity of each and provide additional information, such as the condition of equipment, age, digital vs analogue, Mac or PC, organisation use (OU) vs public access (PA):

Technology	Have	Quantity	Comments
Telephone	☐	_____	_____
Fax	☐	_____	_____
Computer	☐	_____	_____
Printer	☐	_____	_____
Server	☐	_____	_____
Scanner	☐	_____	_____
Internet access	☐	_____	_____
Photocopier	☐	_____	_____
Audio field recorders	☐	_____	_____
Sound studio	☐	_____	_____
Photographic equipment	☐	_____	_____
Video player	☐	_____	_____
Video monitor/TV	☐	_____	_____
Video camera	☐	_____	_____
Video editing suite	☐	_____	_____
Transmitter	☐	_____	_____
Satellite dish	☐	_____	_____
Slide projector	☐	_____	_____
Overhead projector	☐	_____	_____
Silk screening equipment	☐	_____	_____
Other:	☐	_____	_____

59. What other facilities do you have (such as resource centre, meeting room, offices and training room)?

Facility	Contents	Quantity

60. What are your most urgent needs in terms of capital expenditure and the estimated cost?

_____

Appendix

61. What software is your organisation using?

_____
_____

62. Is your organisation using legal software?
Yes ☐   No ☐

63. What software does your organisation need?

_____
_____

64. Does your organisation have a technology plan linked to your business plan?
Yes ☐   No ☐
If yes, please attach.

65. Do you believe there are barriers to technological change in your organisation?
Yes ☐   No ☐
If yes, rank the following barriers in order of importance with 1 being the most important.
Lack of:
Funding for equipment _____
Technology expertise _____
Training _____
Planning _____
Technical services _____
Connectivity _____
Other: _____

66. Who is assisting you with technical matters and how effective is this support?

_____
_____

IX KEY PROBLEM AREAS DEFINED BY THE ORGANISATION

67. Please describe the internal strengths and weaknesses in your organisation:

_____
_____

68. Please describe the external opportunities and threats in the environment you work in:

_____
_____

69. Please make any suggestions on what needs to be done to create a more enabling environment for your organisation to operate in:

_____
_____

THE PEOPLE'S VOICE

Service provider questionnaire

SECTION 1: CONTACT DETAILS

1. Name and position: _____
2. Organisation: _____
3. Postal address: _____
4. Telephone: _____
5. Fax: _____
6. Cell phone: _____
7. E-mail: _____
8. Website: _____

SECTION 2: ORGANISATIONAL DETAILS

9. In what year was your organisation founded? _____

10. What is the legal status of your organisation?
- Statutory body ☐
- Section 21 company ☐
- Trust ☐
- Close Corporation ☐
- Other: ☐

11. What are your organisations core objectives?
- Skills development ☐
- Job creation ☐
- Personal enrichment ☐
- Media diversity ☐
- Development ☐
- Strengthen civil society ☐
- Access to information ☐
- Community cultural development ☐
- Professional development ☐
- Other: _____ ☐

12. What services does your organisation offer?
- Training ☐
- Content development ☐
- Advocacy ☐
- Networking ☐
- Research ☐
- News agency ☐
- Technical support ☐
- Organisational development ☐
- Broadcasting/distribution ☐
- Access to facilities ☐
- Printing ☐

APPENDIX

    SMME support ☐
    Other: _____ ☐

13. What sectors do your programmes cater for?
    Radio ☐
    Video ☐
    Print ☐
    Multimedia ☐
    Visual arts ☐
    Performing arts ☐
    Design ☐
    Technical services ☐
    Other: ☐

14. What is your organisation's target group?
    Previously disadvantaged individuals ☐
    Children (ages 0–12) ☐
    Youth (ages 13–25) ☐
    The aged (over 55 years) ☐
    Women ☐
    People with disabilities ☐
    Unemployed ☐
    Unions ☐
    Schools ☐
    General population ☐
    Churches ☐
    Civic structures ☐
    NGOs ☐
    Other: ☐

15. How do you know what the needs of this target group are? _____

16. What is your organisation's geographical reach? _____

17. Governance (applies to NGOs):
    How many board members do you have? _____
    How is your board comprised (beneficiaries and experts)? _____

    How are board members elected and how long is their term of office? _____

    Name and contact details of the Chairperson of the board? _____

18. Is your organisation a member of any network/oversight body?
    Yes ☐   No ☐
    If yes, please specify _____

THE PEOPLE'S VOICE

19. Does your organisation have partnership with other organisations?
   Yes ☐   No ☐
   If so, please specify below:

Name of organisation	Nature of partnership

SECTION 3: RESOURCES AND FACILITIES

20. How many people does your organisation employ? _____

21. Is your organisation able to accommodate people with disabilities? _____
   If so, in what ways: _____

22. Is your organisation able to offer:
   On-site catering ☐
   On-site accommodation ☐

23. What resources are contained in your on-site facilities (infrastructure and equipment):
   _____
   _____

24. Does your organisation have mobile training facilities? _____
   If so, please specify: _____

25. What was your organisation's approximate budget in 2002? _____

26. Please list your sources of income in 2002 on the table below:

	Source of income	Approximate overall percentage of budget	General comments/ challenges (increase/decrease)
International donor grants			
South African donors			
Government grants			
Corporate social investment			
Self generated income, e.g. private sector/govt. contracts, training fees			

©HSRC 2004

APPENDIX

SECTION 4: TRAINING SERVICE DELIVERY
(applies to organisations that provide training)

27. What is your organisation's level of engagement with the National Skills Development Framework?

Are your courses registered with SAQA?
Yes ☐   No ☐   In progress ☐

Are your training programmes accredited with a Sectoral Education and Training Authority?
Yes ☐   No ☐   In progress ☐

If yes, or in progress, which SETA are you accredited with?
ETDP SETA ☐   MAPPP SETA ☐   Other, please specify: _____

Are you currently paying Skills Development Levies?
Yes ☐   No ☐   In progress ☐

28. What training does your organisation offer?

Course area	Skills acquired	Duration in hours	Target Group

29. How do you deliver training?

Training on-site (in your premises) ☐
Regional or 'clustered' training   On-site ☐   Off-site ☐   ☐
Off-site mentorship by fieldworker ☐
Customised training for individual organisations ☐
Set courses ☐
Other ☐

30. Do you track your clients over time:
Yes ☐   No ☐

31. Do you develop your own learner support materials?
Yes ☐   No ☐

SECTION 5: INFORMATION MANAGEMENT

32. How do you obtain information about developments in your sector? _____
_____

THE PEOPLE'S VOICE

33. How would you like to obtain information about developments in your sector?
_____
_____

34. What information would you like to receive? _____
_____

35. Does your organisation have the following capacity, in terms of information management?

	Yes	In development	No
Electronic databases, please specify:			
Undertake periodic surveys to gather information pertinent to the sector			
Internet-based research			
Build and maintain own website			
Tracking systems			
Brochure			
Other, please specify:			

SECTION 6: MEDIA DEVELOPMENT AND DIVERSITY: CHALLENGES, STRATEGIES AND ROLES

36. What are the key CHALLENGES facing the MDDA in fulfilling its role to promote media development and diversity in SA? _____
_____
_____
_____

37. What KEY STRATEGIES should the MDDA adopt in order to address these challenges? _____
_____
_____

APPENDIX

38. How do you see the ROLES of the following stakeholders in terms of promoting media development and diversity?

MDDA

National network/s

Service providers

Other:
e.g. Department of Communications

Many thanks for taking time to fill in this questionnaire.

The people's voice

REFERENCES

African Charter on Broadcasting (2001) http://www.misgnet.org/broadcast.html

Aldridge M (1997) Local Sounds, Local Visions: The Struggle for Community Television in South Africa, Paper presented at the Identities, Democracy, Culture and Communication in South Africa Conference. University of Natal, Durban

Aldridge M (2003) *Community Television Broadcasting in South Africa: Theoretical Overview and Business Plan.* http://www.mediastream.co.za/Professional/Loc_tv.html

Andersen B (1983) *Imagined Communities.* London: Verso Press

AEJMC (Association for Education in Journalism and Mass Communication) (2000) *IT: Implications for the Future of Journalism and Mass Communication Education – Final Report of the Subcommittee on Educational Strategies and Technology Change.* http://www.aejmc.org

Benjamin P (2001) Telecentres and Universal Capability: A Study of the Telecentre Programme of the Universal Service Agency in South Africa, 1996–2000. PhD thesis, Aalberg University, Netherlands

Benjamin P & Dahms M (1999) Community: Universal Service and Universal Access Issues, Paper presented at Telia Telecoms in Society Seminar, June 1999, Sweden http://www.communitysa.org.za

Berger G (1996) What is the Community Media? Paper presented at the Community Voices Conference, October 6–11, Malawi. http://www.journ.ru.ac.za/research

Berger G (2000) *Independent Media in South Africa*, Research paper. http://www.journ.ru.ac.za/research

Boafo KST (ed.) (2000) *Promoting Community Media in Africa.* Paris: Unesco

Broadcasting Policy Technical Task Team (1998) Discussion document on broadcasting policy. IBA/Icasa. http://www.icasa.org.za

Burkett I (2003) The Challenges of Building 'Real' and 'Virtual' Human Communities in the 21st Century, In *Encyclopedia of Life Support Systems.* Paris: Unesco

Calabrese A (1991) The Periphery in the Centre: the Information Age and the 'Good Life' in Rural America, *Gazette* 48: 105–128

Cholmondeley CH (2000) The Development of Community Media in the Caribbean, In KST Boafo (ed.) *Promoting Community Media in Africa.* Paris: Unesco

CRIS (Communication Rights in the Information Society) (2002) *Is the Information Society a Useful Concept for Civil Society?* Research paper. http://www.crisinfo.org/live/index.php

CRIS (2002) *What is the Special Significance of Community Media to Civil Society?* Research paper. http://www.crisinfo.org/live/index.php

CRIS (2003) *Contesting the Spectrum Allocation Giveaway*, Research paper. http://www.crisinfo.org/live/index.php

Community Multimedia Services Task Team (2003) *Community Multimedia Services Task Team Report.* Pretoria: Department of Communications

Department of Communications (2001) *Community Electronic Multimedia Indaba Conference Report.* Pretoria: Department of Communications

Development Bank of SA (2003) *An Information Policy Handbook for Southern Africa: A Knowledge Base for Decision-Makers.* http://www.dbsa.org.za/publications/ictpolsa/index.html

Dooms P (2002) *The Licensing of Community Radio: Responses from Stations*, FXI research paper. FXI. http://www.fxi.org.za

Duncan J (ed) (1996) *Between Speech and Silence: Hate Speech, Pornography and the New South Africa.* FXI. http://www.fxi.org.za/public/html

Duncan J & Seleoane M (eds) (1998) *Media and Democracy in South Africa.* Pretoria: HSRC & FXI

Emdon C (2001) Report commissioned by the board of the Independent Media Diversity Trust for the period January 1999 to December 2000

Emdon C (2002) Hungry Jackals: Key Issues About the Rules of Ownership and Control, Foreign Investment and the Licensing of Radio Stations, *Journal of Marketing*, 8 (6): 24–26

Fraser C & Restrepo-Estrada S (2002) Community Radio for Change and Development, *Development* 45 (4): 69–73

FXI (Freedom of Expression Institute) (2002) *2001/2002 Annual Report.* http://www.fxi.org.za

FXI (2002) *Media Law Briefing.* November 1996. http://www.fxi.org.za

GCIS (Government Communication and Information Services) (2001) *Multi-purpose Community Centres: Business Plan Document.* http://www.gcis.gov.za

GCIS (2002) *A Conceptual Framework: The Role of Multi-Media Centres in the Development of the Media.* Work-in-progress. 27 November 2002 http://www.gcis.gov.za

Gibbs C (1995) Big Help for Small Papers, *Quill* 83 (2): 32

REFERENCES

GCIS (2000) *Media Diversity and Development Agency Position Paper* (draft) http://www.gcis.gov.za

Hadland A & Voorbach H (2003) Evaluation of the Core Courses of the Institute for the Advancement of Journalism, Report. Cape Town: Human Sciences Research Council

Hagg G (2002) *Towards Optimally Functioning Community Arts Centres in South Africa*, Report on a national audit of community arts centres. Pretoria: Department of Arts and Culture

Hindman DB (1996) Community Newspapers, Community Structural Pluralism and Local Conflict with Non-Local groups, *J&MC Quarterly*, 73(3): 708–721

Hollander E (1992) The Emergence of Small-Scale Media, In Jankowski N et al. (eds) *The People's Voice: Local Radio and Television in Europe*, Academia Research Monograph 6. London: John Libbey

Howley K (2003) Topic Overview of Community Media, In *St James Encyclopedia of Popular Culture*. http://www.findarticles.com/g1epc/tov/2419100276/p1/article.html

IBA (Independent Broadcasting Authority) (2000) Submission to the SAHRC on Racism and the Media. 11 February 2000. http://www.iba.org.za/racism/html

Icasa (Independent Communications Authority of South Africa) (March 1999) *Position paper on a Definition of Advertising, the Regulation of Infomercials and the Regulation of Programme Sponsorship*. http://www.icasa.org.za

Icasa (April 1999) *Discussion Paper on Satellite Broadcasting*. http://www.icasa.org.za

Icasa (April 1999) *Position Paper on Revision of IBA Code of Conduct*. http://www.icasa.org.za

Icasa (September 1999) *Position Paper on Self-Help Stations*. http://www.icasa.org.za

Icasa (July 2000) *Submission on MDDA Bill*. http://www.icasa.org.za

Icasa (December 2000) *Discussion Paper on Review of Local Content Quotas*. http://www.icasa.org.za

Jacobs S (n.d.) Media and Policy Debates in Post-Apartheid South Africa, Unpublished PhD thesis. Birkbeck College, University of London

Jankowski N, Prehn O & Stappers J (eds) (1992) *The People's Voice: Local Radio and Television in Europe*, Academia Research Monograph 6. London: John Libbey

Karikari K (2000) The Development of Community Media in French-speaking West Africa, In KST Boafo (ed.) *Promoting Community Media in Africa*. Paris: Unesco

Klein HK (1999) Making It Happen Now, *Peace Review* 11(1): 41–53

Louw PE (ed) (1993) *South African Media Policy: Debates of the 1990s*. Cape Town: Anthropos Publishers

Lundby K (1992) Community TV as a Tool of Local Culture. In Jankowski N et al. *The People's Voice: Local Radio and Television in Europe*, Academia Research Monograph 6. London: John Libbey

Maitland Company Law Firm (2003) Investing in South Africa – Media and Commercial Law, Keynote address: Media Freedom Seminar. http://www.maitlandco.com

Majozi M Community Media in South Africa, In KST Boafo (ed.) *Promoting Community Media in Africa*. Paris: Unesco

NISCC (National Intersectoral Steering Committee) (2001) *An Implementation Framework for MPCCs in South Africa*. 24 September 2001. http://www.gcis.gov.za

Naughton T (1999) The Need for and Role of a Media Development Agency, FXI research document. http://www.fxi.org.za

Nell M & Shapiro J (2001) *Community Radio Training Evaluation: First Footprints of the African Renaissance 1997–2001*. Cape Town: British Council & Open Society Foundation

Netshitenzhe J (1998) Keynote address. Media Freedom Seminar. 19 October 1998. http://www.gcis.gov.za

Ninan S (2000) What is the Status of Community Radio, Newspapers and Television in India? *Unesco Courier* February 2000 53 (2): 31

Non-Aligned Movement (1998) Information and Communication, In *The Final Document of the XIIth Summit*. Durban, 2–3 September. http://www.nam.gov.za/xii summit

Opubor AE (2000) The Development of Community Media in East and Southern Africa, In KST Boafo *Promoting Community Media in Africa*. Paris: Unesco

PDU (Print Development Unit) (2002) *New Markets, New Readers, New Publishers: The Rise of Entrepreneurial Community Newspapers and Magazines in South Africa*. Johannesburg: Johnnic Publishing

Scott C (1997) Democracy, Development and Community Television: A dream or a Vision? *Democracy Watch* 1: http://www.csls.org.za/webcon/ARTID.html

Siemering B (1997) *The Many Voices of Community Radio*. Geneva: World Bank EDI Forum

Sparks A (2003) *Beyond the Miracle*. London: Profile Books

Steenveld L (ed) (2002) *Training for Media Transformation and Democracy – A Colloquium for South African Journalists, Media Trainers and Media Scholars*. Johannesburg: Sanef, Independent Newspapers & Rhodes University

References

Stevens J (n.d.) Unbundling the word 'Community'. Fourth year Journalism Paper, Rhodes University. http://www.journ.ru.ac.za/research

Stevenson T (2002) Communities of Tomorrow, *Futures* 34: 735–744

Stretton N (2002) Print Media Partnerships, In L Steenveld (ed.) *Training for Media Transformation and Democracy – A Colloquium for South African Journalists, Media Trainers and Media Scholars.* Johannesburg: Sanef, Independent Newspapers & Rhodes University

Tabung L (2000) The Development of Community Media in South-East Asia, In KST Boafo (ed.) *Promoting Community Media in Africa.* Unesco: Paris

Thorne K (1996) Where is the Money Going to Come From? In S Sorensen & K Thorne (eds) *Voices and Visions: Audiovisual Media in the New South Africa:* Denmark: Zebra Information Office

Thorne K (1998) Community Media: A Price We Can Afford? In J Duncan & M Seleoane (eds) *Media and Democracy in South Africa.* Pretoria: HSRC & FXI

Thorne K (2002) Beyond Rhetoric: Community Media for Sustainable Development, Paper presented at the Highway Africa Conference, Nemisa, Johannesburg

Tleane C (2002) Hung in the Sky: The Impact of Licensing Delays on Community Radio Stations, FXI research paper. FXI. http://www.fxi.org.za

Tomaselli, K & Dunn H (eds) (2001) *Media, Democracy and Renewal in Southern Africa.* Colorado Springs: International Academic Publications

Tsedu M, Wrotlesley S & Clay P (2002) Sanef's 2002 South African National Journalism Skills Audit: An introduction, *Ecquid Novi* 23 (1): 5–10

Unesco (1989) Communication in the Service of Humanity, Document from Records of the General Conference, 25th Session, October-November 2002, Paris

Urgoiti G (ed.) (1999) *Community Radio Manual.* Open Society Foundation. http://www.osf.org.za

Van Eijk N (1992) The Legal and Policy Aspects of Community Broadcasting, In N Jankowski, O Prehn & J Stappers (eds) *The People's Voice: Local Radio and Television in Europe,* Academia Research Monograph 6. London: John Libbey

Wanyeki LM (2000) The Development of Community Media in English-speaking West Africa, In KST Boafo (ed) *Promoting Community Media in Africa.* Paris: Unesco

Windhoek Declaration on Promoting an Independent and Pluralistic African Press (1991) http://www.misanet.org/charters/windhoek.html